". . . is one of the best books written on the contemporary disorder known as 'The Teen-Ager' and the infective source of disorder—his parents. It ought to be required reading for every teen-ager and every parent, for the problem that the contemporary teen-ager presents to himself, his parents, and his society has attained such dimensions, that it can continue to be overlooked only at our own peril."

—Ashley Montagu

"This lively, well-documented, and by no means unsympathetic discussion of teen-age culture, its effects on those who practice it, and its influence on American society, can be read with as much interest—and profit —by teen-agers themselves as by their elders. It is a book for all ages, dealing forthrightly with a universal problem central to the happiness of all."

—A. Whitney Griswold
President, Yale University

". . . a thoughtful interpretation of the teen-age world and a fascinating description of it. This is a book for adults, including parents and teachers, but it ought to be read by teen-agers, too."

—Saturday Review

"This four-fisted attack on teen-age tyranny . . . will elicit 'hallelujahs' from worried adults . . . punchy, stimulating, formidable . . . Parents, arise, and throw off your yoke!"

—Los Angeles Times

Teen-Age Tyranny

BY GRACE AND FRED M. HECHINGER

A CREST REPRINT

FAWCETT PUBLICATIONS, INC., GREENWICH, CONN.
MEMBER OF AMERICAN BOOK PUBLISHERS COUNCIL, INC.

A Crest Book published by arrangement with
William Morrow & Company

Grateful acknowledgment is made to Leonard Bernstein and
Stephen Sondheim for permission to quote (on page 156) from
the lyrics of *West Side Story*, copyright © 1957 by
Leonard Bernstein and Stephen Sondheim; and to Free Press of
Glencoe for permission to quote, on various pages, from
The Adolescent Society, by James S. Coleman,
copyright © 1961 by The Free Press, A Corporation.

PRINTING HISTORY
First Morrow printing, January 1963
Second printing, April 1963
Third printing, July 1963

An alternate selection of The Kiplinger Book Service, February 1963

First Crest printing, April 1964

Crest Books are published by Fawcett World Library,
67 West 44th Street, New York, New York 10036.
Printed in the United States of America.

To Paul
Our own future teen-ager

Contents

Introduction

Teen-age, like birth and death, is inevitable. It is nothing to be ashamed of. Nor is it a badge of special distinction worthy of a continuous birthday party. And while teen-agers should be afforded mitigating circumstances for some of their actions and views, on the basis of natural immaturity, they should neither be placed in an aquarium tank for purposes of exhibition and analysis nor be put on a pedestal to be extolled for that admittedly enviable condition—youth.

Without appearing defensive, we want to avoid unnecessary argument later on by putting our cards on the table. We are not against teen-agers, nor are we particularly for them. It would be dishonest for us to claim that some of our best friends are teen-agers, though some of our best friends have them. We make no secret of the fact that we were teen-agers once. We remember it well, though by teen-age standards it was a long time ago.

We are not writing this book to declare war on teen-agers or to put the clock back to the days when children were supposed to be seen but not heard. And while we have some specific and uninhibited views about present dating and mating habits of teen-agers, we stand ready to deny the charge that we yearn for family-arranged marriages and finishing-school chaperones.

What worries us is not the greater freedom of youth but rather the abdication of the rights and privileges of adults for the convenience of the immature. We believe teen-age should be regarded as a phase of human development, with both pleasant and unpleasant side effects, rather than as either an achievement or a disease. The pages which follow, therefore, are not intended as a declaration of war but as an honest attempt to make "the teens" once again a transition period to full man- or womanhood rather than a tribal "subculture"; a temporary condition to be terminated with normal speed rather than to be artificially induced and prolonged like the life of a hothouse plant; a time of growth to be treated with understanding and even indulgence but not with unlimited license.

We do not want to be cantankerous. But we strongly believe that, for reasons to be documented in the succeeding chapters, American civilization tends to stand in such awe of its teen-age segment that it is in danger of becoming a teen-age society, with permanently teen-age standards of thought, culture and goals. As a result, American society is growing down rather than growing up.

This is a creeping disease, not unlike hardening of the arteries. It is a softening of adulthood. It leads to immature goals in music, art and literature. It forces newspapers, television producers and movie-makers to translate the adult English usage into the limited vocabulary of the teen-culture. It opens up vast opportunities for commercial exploitation and thereby sets off a chain reaction which constantly strengthens teen-age tyranny.

It is a tyranny that dominates most brutally the teen-agers themselves. What starts with relatively innocent conforming to the ways of the crowd soon turns into manipulation of those crowd mores by a combination of inept adult leadership and plain commercial exploitation. The longer it continues, the harder it becomes, as in the case of every artifically imposed regime, for dissenters to declare their independence.

We are fully aware that not all teen-agers and their parents have fallen victim to teen-age tyranny. Many have retained their freedom and upheld their standards. But even those who have resisted the trend know that the stronger the tide the harder it becomes to move against it. We hope that our efforts will make it a little easier for them.

One final word of preface: we are not concerned with juvenile delinquency, except where it becomes part of the "general" behavior of a substantial number of teen-agers. The reason we will not deal with delinquency here is that we strongly feel this to be a different and special problem. It should be treated as such, and by experts far better equipped to diagnose and combat it.

It might be charged that our observations deal entirely with middle-class America and its teen-agers. The slant, if it is to be so labeled, is deliberate. We are fully aware that the mores and the problems of the underprivileged are quite different.

But the truth of the matter is that ours is a society in which middle-class values set the pace and determine "normal" behavior patterns. The slum family of today, whether immigrant or racially oppressed, wants nothing so much as to be graduated into the middle-class way of life.

This is why we have confined our scrutiny to the ways of middle-class teen-agers—without apology. They are setting the patterns. They are the models for those who after them will cope with the business of growing up.

1 *Learning to Be Teen-Agers*

The American teen-ager is brought up in a world of baffling conflicts and contradictions. No society has ever been more protective of its children. American youngsters are given the best medical care. They are fed according to the latest nutritional dictates, with abundance, if not overabundance. Obesity has replaced malnutrition as a serious problem. Teen-agers are offered the advantages of universal education. They are protected, by law, against being made to work until they are well beyond their middle teens.

Yet, despite the protective shield against physical harm or hurt, they are exposed to the most questionable aspects of adult society with a minimum of protection—much less, in fact, than is provided for the young in countries which offer their children far fewer advantages. For a number of reasons, ranging from the purely commercial profit-motive to the misguided interpretation of freedom, no motion picture, no matter how unsuitable, is effectively made off-limits to minors. The worst excesses of crime and violence are made easily accessible to children on television and in print. The adult world's frustrated and juvenile obsession with sex saturates the adolescent world with inescapable and distorted images.

Yet, the political speech-making and educational sermonizing stresses such phrases as "moral and spiritual values" in a way that makes them appear to be a commodity to be bought and delivered, quite apart from the realities of life. Remnants of Puritanism create fictitious standards, such as the Blue Laws, which are written into the statute books without being given any concrete or sensible meaning.

Children are still reared on talk about the morality of thrift and saving for a rainy day, while they are surrounded by signs urging their elders to "Fly Now, Pay Later."

No nation's youth has ever been given a better insight into the ways of science and the machinery of their own bodies. Yet, the spiel of the medicine man and of the cure-all side show has been given vast network billing, and the same youngsters who understand intricate rocket technology are confronted everywhere with diagrams and "scientific" cartoons intended to make them believe totally false and meaningless "facts" about the scientific powers of products ranging from laxatives to floor wax.

The majority of American states have ordered their schools to "teach" the dangers of alcohol and narcotics. Yet, the cocktail party is the ultimate form of social respectability and the legal approach to the narcotics problem is nothing short of medieval.

If we accept the premise (and no other premise holds out any hope for change and improvement) that education is the foundation of human activity and progress, then any look at the American teen-ager must begin with a review of the education and general upbringing he has been given.

Today's teen-agers are the sons and daughters of parents brought up in the heyday of the America of progressive education and permissive child-rearing. They are offspring of the generation which had seen the United States at the zenith of its power, at once self-confident and self-centered. The world was then America's oyster. Political isolationism was pragmatically justifiable by the nation's self-sufficiency and military security.

The spokesmen for progressive education in the twenties and thirties could afford the luxury of worrying only about the preferences and desires of the individual child. They gloried in their revolution against the regimented old schools which had imposed adult standards on children and had, in fact, considered youngsters largely as small grownups. They triumphantly and effectively joined forces with the psychologists, who had also come into their own, and they drove home the vital point that a teacher who knew something about the processes of a child's mind could inspire almost spontaneous learning.

It was an era of educational optimism. If every child only fulfilled himself, the total of fulfilled selves would give society plenty of talent of any and every kind. To think of the needs of society, much less of the "state," was not only unnecessary; in progressive and democratic terms (and the two came to be synonymous), it was reactionary and anti-social.

"Self-expression" was one of the magic words of the period. It was (and ought to remain) a good and important word. It was the opposite of the kind of child-rearing and education which made dull repetition, imitation and memorization the core of learning. Coupled with the psychological revolution, self-expression was to be the initial and important antidote to regimented, meaningless rote learning.

Where there was real talent, self-expression had the great advantage of increasing the chances of its discovery. The trouble started when all forms of self-expression were put on an equal level of importance and value. The child who just smeared paints across the pad was seen as expressing himself as usefully as the child who showed the beginnings of a sense of color and pattern. Were not both letting the individual soul speak? And who was to pass value judgment on the expressions of those sacred individuals?

The youngster who had something original to say was given no more recognition than the classmate who merely babbled for the sake of the sound of his voice or, worse, his quickly recognized power to gain attention and disrupt the show. Utlimately, this view led to the extreme perversion of the progressive idea—the theory that ungrammatical idiom is just as good and as expressive of the real self as correct usage. In fact, there were some who began to deride the "correct" expression as society-dictated and therefore destructive of individual expression.

The second magic word—first cousin to "self-expression" —was "child-centered."

Here again, the original intent was sound. Teaching the pupil anything, from Latin to home economics, has very little value unless it makes sense to the child and responds to the child's comprehension and scope. In this interpretation, then, making the child the center of the lesson is little more than restating the purpose of the school: to educate the child. Simple as this premise may seem, it needed restating: there were too many teachers who, because they were frustrated or second-rate scholars, were more interested in their own notion of the integrity of their subject and specialty than in the proper teaching of children.

Trouble came when the sound idea of the "child-centered" school was combined with the permissive doctrine of extreme self-expression. From it follows the equation of individualism with selfishness. It is one thing to say that the purpose of the school is to teach the child, but quite another to let the child dominate the school and the curriculum. The early progressives insisted that the curriculum make sense to the child and that the content of education be adjusted to the age, maturity and comprehension of the pupil. The perversion of this sound doctrine came when this was equated with the child's likes and dislikes.

Dr. John H. Fischer, President of Teachers College, Columbia University, defined the schools' task as succinctly as possible: "Schools are established by adults to give young people the advantage of systematic teaching and learning." This tells the entire story. It puts the adults clearly in a position of leadership and responsibility and it places stress on an important priority in education and child-rearing: systematic action.

Obviously, this rules out the child's domination of his own upbringing and education. It implies that a superior experience and broader view of the world and of the child's future must determine what is to be done and left undone. This leaves the child in the center of the parents' and teachers' concern but not in the center of the controls. While an excellent case can be made that as much as possible of what a child is made to learn should be tested by him in practice, it does not follow that everything must be learned through trial and error. There are some errors that can be avoided through reasoned demonstration or explanation by older persons. There are other errors which must be prevented by outright prohibition, if for no other reason than the protection of the child's safety. It is relatively easy to get agreement, for instance, that a child must not cross the street against the lights, regardless of the child's preferences. It ought to be equally acceptable to have teen-agers live up to certain rules of sexual behavior, without putting them to the practical test. Yet, there seems to be little agreement on adult authority to determine how young people ought to behave or what they should study, and when, or on the extent to which, they should or should not dominate the household.

Translated into the more technical aspects of schooling, the idea of permissiveness has led to a system of "elective" subjects in many schools. In the worst instances, the selection of courses was left pretty much to the whims and rationalizations of youngsters; in the more modified instances of schools with guidance specialists, a certain amount of order was brought into the chaos by way of persuasion.

What the extreme advocates of the child-centered school

and of permissiveness in child-rearing and education overlooked was the effect of excessive responsibility on youngsters in making choices without the benefit of experience. Making decisions is probably the toughest task that faces human beings, regardless of age. The mark of the successful executive is exactly that ability, and the problem never becomes an easy one. It is an impossible one without the prerequisite of experience and knowledge, plus the prior mapping out of goals of conduct and targets of achievement. To make decisions, we must know the alternatives and where they lead, in addition to knowing where we want to go, and where others have gone before us.

To ignore this basic relationship between knowledge and action or between experience and decision-making is to launch young people on ships without sails or rudders. It condemns them to indirection and drift. In the adult world, we readily acknowledge that the pressure to make decisions or take action without the proper intellectual or moral preparation is one of the major causes for failure and mental breakdowns. While the immediate effects on children are not as drastic (only because the child is not held equally responsible for the consequences of his action for him and those around him), the long-term results are insecurity and lack of purpose.

The classic joke about progressive education is that of the child asking the teacher: "Gee! Do we have to do again what we want to do?" It is a classic that bears repeating because it cuts so close to the bone. It exposes the fact that freedom to do what we want to do becomes meaningful only when we know what we want.

Without education and training, the option to do what we want to do is a relatively empty one. There is a devastating parallel between the progressive education joke and the American G.I. in such centers of culture and activity as, say, London and Paris. Although their pockets are filled with money and every opportunity and privilege is extended to them, the number of soldiers who are bored and at a loss to know what to do is appalling. Nor does this apply only to the American in uniform. The American tourist abroad or even at home is not far different. The invention of the "social director" in American hotels and resorts gives ample testimony that even the adult who lacks background and training does not want just to be permitted to do what he wants to do. He wants to be told, directed, pushed.

For the adult to need such direction and guidance is disgraceful. For the child, it is natural. It is only when the child is not given direction and, in Dr. Fischer's terms, "the advantage of systematic teaching and learning" that the teenager and the adult end up by being aimless.

Closely related to this invitation to drift is the peculiar misinterpretation of "democratic living." Possibly as a reaction to the terrible example of perverted leadership abroad, in a long succession of Fascist and Communist dictatorships, American education and child-rearing experts discredited all leadership, including that traditionally provided for young people and children by adults. The committee form of action and decision-making replaced the leadership principle. It was not at all unusual for children, even in the early grades of school, to vote on the day's activities. The very image of a teacher's place at the head of the class was depicted as authoritarian and reactionary. Instead, the teacher was urged to be a "pal" to the children. Classes often worked and played in small groups, each organized as a committee. The teacher acted as a "resource person" or adviser. In all instances of disagreement, a vote settled the uncertainty.

In a not atypical teacher-training class at a good liberal arts college, a few years ago, the students could be observed discussing for over half an hour what they wanted to study in seminar that morning. Even after they had made the decision, based on no other priorities than their own guesses and preferences, the discussion went on almost without any participation by the teacher. Yet, the teacher was known to all, including the students, to be a woman of great experience and extensive knowledge. It is not surprising that future teachers, themselves conditioned to this waste of a teacher's knowledge and talents will perpetuate the nonleadership concept in their own classrooms later on.

The story is told of a nature class in third grade. The children are shown a rabbit, and after a while a discussion starts as to whether it is a boy rabbit or a girl rabbit. When there appears to be considerable disagreement, one little boy, obviously familiar with the ways of modern education, raises his hand and suggests: "Let's take a vote."

Substituting discussion and agreement—a pooling of ignorance—for the study of facts is one of the deficiencies which comes home to roost in teen-age. Listening to elementary school students debating ideas they cannot understand may be considered cute; the same practice repeated in teen-age and later is deplorable. A recent television show which captured some of the best approaches to teaching in today's schools showed a group of elementary school children discussing matters of war, politics and world affairs in complete absence of any factual information. This conditions them to the practice of forming opinions without the benefit of facts.

Finally, but most important, a strange contradiction has been built into the American system of child development and education. While intellectual development has been slowed down to a pace more leisurely than would be acceptable in any other society, social growth has been subjected to a forced, hothouse-plant speed-up which takes on dangerous and absurd proportions. This is comparable to putting into harness together a fast race horse and a lame nag.

Take the academic side of the American school. "Readiness" has been the motto. It is, of course, an important element in the handling of children everywhere. In nontechnical terms, it simply means that every step in a child's early learning must be taken at the right moment and after the way has been properly prepared.

Infants pretty much take care of readiness by themselves. They progress from one stage to another—sitting up, standing, walking, talking, etc.—as they are ready for it. In fact, if there is one similarity of behavior among all normal infants, it is their impatience to move from one accomplishment to another, each accompanied by a great deal of constant effort and followed by a marvelous joy over successful conquest of another hurdle.

In the early days of the progressive school reforms of the twenties, educators appeared to take cognizance of this natural and orderly development of children's readiness to cope with more and more difficult problems. They realized, for instance, that the traditional elementary school primers were intended to be embarrassing obstacle courses which made it their almost sadistically adult-oriented business to make children stumble, to prove to them that they knew little or nothing. Under this absurd scheme of things children were asked to read sentences that meaninglessly strung together rare and polysyllabic words. Even if the children knew how to "read" those words, they could not possibly understand their meaning, and if they obediently looked them up in the dictionary, the exercise was sterile and without purpose. Neither in speech nor good literature would they soon again encounter the mysterious words whose mastery made reading a dreary sort of intellectual gymnastics rather than a joyful extension of that discovery which had made the same children crow with delight, in their days of babyhood, when they discovered that sounds could be built into words which mother and father understood.

But soon the modern educators, in their effort to adjust the material for learning, and discovery to the minds of children, made the same mistake in reverse which their adult-minded predecessors had made earlier: they misunderstood the children's interests and capacities. While the earlier group had purposely overestimated the capacities of children, those who followed tended, though unintentionally, to underestimate them. While the traditional school had attempted to cram precocious knowledge into the minds of pupils, the new educators postponed challenge to a point where learning became meaningless and dull because it no longer involved discovery.

Here again, the business of words—the currency of all learning—offers the best example. Having banished the abuse of word-gymnastics from the early reading exercises, the educators built a braking mechanism into the books manufactured for children. Word lists became strait jackets rather than guides, and since the new pseudo scientists of education tended to work in close harmony and agreement, the word lists were marked by a sameness which could only turn into regimentation of authors.

Entire primers or readers were concocted with a total of fewer than twenty words, repeated endlessly. These were the books that led to the now familiar joke about the elementary school teacher who, starting out to work in the morning, wrapped her fender around the garage door. She got out of the car, surveyed the damage and said: "Look look look, oh oh oh, damn damn damn." Recently, when a father of a first-grader told the story to a group of friends, unaware that Junior was listening, the little boy said solemnly: "That's from the book we're reading in school, but we haven't come to 'damn' yet."

The point is that the children's vocabulary is way ahead of those laborious technicians of modern education who, though studiously child-oriented, have lost contact with real children. Perhaps the story about the two tots who, during recess, discuss the intricacies of solid-fuel rockets and, at the sound of the bell, look up and say, "Okay, let's go back to stringing those beads again," is apocryphal; but it is close to the mark in spoofing the lag between the interests of real children and the excessively protective, slow progress mapped out by the early-childhood educationists.

Letting children advance "at their own pace" was another of the slogans of the child psychologists who were justly alarmed over the adult-oriented curriculum of the "old" school. But in the hands of unimaginative and dull people the pace became merely unimaginative and dull. It ceased to bear any more relationship to the children's "own" speed than had the earlier chasing of ephemeral academic butterflies.

The story of early reading is, of course, merely a symptom of a philosophy. As these children moved from the elementary grades into high school, the overprotection and tasteless spoon-feeding continued. At each stage, in the interest of making learning easy or (the term that has become the coat of arms of modern life) "fun," much of the stamina and starch was taken out of the material to be learned. In such fields as economics, history and geography, where controversies of ideas and theories require searching and painstaking analysis, the textbooks were prettied up with illustrations but drained of challenge to the intellect. In many high schools, where good and demanding courses were still being offered, they were made optional, with the result that they became the domain of only a small, exceptional group rather than the testing ground for the mass of young people.

"Postponement" became an educational principle. In order to avoid pushing young minds beyond their capacity, pupils were permitted and, at least indirectly, often encouraged to postpone what was clearly grade school learning until junior high and high school days.

Simultaneously with the permissive attitude toward the development of the intellect, American schools and society appeared to be almost perversely determined to rush the youngsters' social development. In a recent issue of the National Education Association Journal an elementary school principal complained, not at all atypically: "I don't like it, but my P.T.A. wants me to have fifth- and sixth-grade dances, and sometimes the fourth grade is invited to even out the number of boys and girls." Mothers beam when their seven-year-olds "pair-off," just as their mothers may have beamed, according to different standards of that generation, when children, at the same age, were able to recite a poem or write a legible postcard. A school psychologist reports that in many communities "dating" is an approved activity for nine-year-olds simply because this is considered essential training for junior high school.

Much more will be said about dating habits of modern teen-agers in another chapter, but the problems created by the educational conflict between intellectual "postponement" (if not actual retardation) and social rushing must be understood as a key to the problems of American teen-agers. The problem is symbolized by two inventions of modern American education: automatic promotion and the junior high school. In fairness to the recuperative powers of American society and to hope for the future, it must be added that both are increasingly under scrutiny and, in many places, are undergoing revision.

The principle of automatic promotion, or not keeping any youngster back in grade, was based on the premise that it is psychologically unsound to keep older students in the same class with younger ones. The sense of failure and inferiority engendered among those who have thus been left behind was feared to hurt these children psychologically.

While this fear is well founded in extreme instances, it is significant that the same fear was not expressed concerning those youngsters who, having been unable to master the intellectual content and requirement of the previous grade, have been advanced along with their classmates in the interest of their sociological or chronological development. There is, in this very procedure, a strong hint of the double standard concerning the importance of the intellectual and the social aspects of education. For some reason, the fear that the youngster who reaches junior high school without the ability to read properly might be saddled with feelings of inferiority seems to trouble educators far less than the fear that the same child, asked to repeat a grade, might be offended by the social implications of remaining with a younger group. That this double standard can be dangerous has been borne out by the startling regularity with which delinquency and inability to read appear to coincide.

The idea of the junior high school was cut out of the same ideological cloth as the concept of automatic promotion. It was created for social rather than intellectual reasons. Its founders argued that, since adolescents in their early teens have different social problems from those of grade school children and senior high school students, they ought to be kept apart—protected—from both. Although the supporters of this idea naturally argued that the aim was to give the junior high school students a better opportunity to develop according to their special needs, the consequence was to place them into something of an isolation ward. This may have given them "protection" of a sort, but it also reinforced their special problems by putting them into a test tube.

In many ways, this is typical of the American interpretation of the teen-age problem. Instead of making adolescence a transition period, necessary and potentially even valuable (if often slightly comical), it began to turn it into a separate way of life to be catered to, exaggerated and extended far beyond its biological duration. Eventually it became a way of life imitated by young and not-so-young adults.

This normalized an abnormality. It gave teen-age an air, not of matter-of-fact necessity, but of special privilege and admiration. Instead of giving teen-agers a sense of growing up, it created the impression that the rest of society had a duty to adjust its ways and its standards to teen-culture, without realizing that "teen-culture" is an absurd contradiction of irreconcilable terms.

Educationally it was inevitable that, if the early teens were offered an institutional empire of their own, they would be tempted to build for themselves a society which, since it was vague about intellectual values, would single out for special attention and imitation the most trivial aspects of upper-teen and young adult life. When Dr. James B. Conant surveyed the junior high schools, he was understandably scandalized by the overemphasis on athletics, marching bands and cap-and-gown commencement exercises, not to mention proms and dances, and in extreme cases, secret societies, fraternities and sororities. In addition to making the schools of the early teens unnecessarily top-heavy on the side of the extraneous trappings and social activities, this also gave impetus to another characteristic difficulty: youngsters were offered too much, too soon, at a stage of their lives at which they can derive only superficial enjoyment from activities that ought to give real pleasure to them later on. The effect is growing boredom with things which ought to be exciting—a social aging before their time.

A high school commencement can and should be an occasion of importance and meaning. It is a goal. All effective goals should be surrounded by an aura of awe and cloaked in a veil of doubt about their attainability. There is little satisfaction in aiming at a target that is so close and so familiar that anybody can score a bull's-eye, without skill, training or suspense. Would any explorer think it worth his while to set out on an expedition without hidden obstacles? A vain German king is said to have had divers hook huge fishes to his line underwater in order to impress his subjects. How many real fishermen would find any satisfaction from such easy certainty of success?

Yet, the junior high school commencement is exactly such a device: it puts the sure catch of an academic honor on every student's hook. In the process, it pushes the real achievement of the high school diploma off the traditional pedestal of desirable solemnity. In fact, the downgrading of the symbols of achievement creates so irresistible a chain reaction that there are now elementary schools—and even kindergartens—which indulge in cap-and-gown graduation ceremonies.

Even more serious, though less obvious, is the cheerleader and drum majorette cult which, fairly objectionable on the college scene, is downright obscene in the junior high and high school milieu. With their heavy overtones of sexual exhibitionism, the drilling, strutting examples of adolescent leg art caused *Time* magazine to label them, not inaccurately, the "nymphettes."

"For every struggling, prancing, stick-swinging, tail-twitching majorette in the nation, there are about 100 or so others who would give every Bobby Darin record they own to get on the squad," *Time* said. And, the report added, "the searing competition carries into home and family," with mothers urging their teen-age daughters to practice their phony chorus-line smiles and assemble their spangled bathing-beauty costumes which may cost as much as $100.

Colleges, instead of keeping things on an even, civilized keel, often make things worse by offering scholarships for, of all things, talented baton-twirlers. Naturally, they put an educational label on this as on all other habitual aberrations. They call it body-building and the key to slim-figured poise. Probably as much could be said for a vigorous strip-tease exercise.

Even more serious, though less obvious, is the effect of the junior high school isolation on intellectual progress. Based on avoidance of harmful academic pressures, the junior high school was intended to serve as a buffer between the playful approach to learning in the elementary grades and the more serious academic aims of the "real" high school.

In practice, the result often was a close parallel to the "getting ready" ritual between kindergarten and first grade. "Reading readiness," for instance, assumed that children were unable to cope with such simple ideas as "right" and "left," "in" and "out," "up" and "down." And while it may have been important to provide such understanding for the few children who came to school without it, belaboring such basic and (once mastered) boring concepts merely took the excitement out of learning for the majority of children. By the same token, the youngster who completes elementary school and moves to the next higher level is severely let down if the junior high school, by overplaying its protective "buffer" function, gives the student the impression that nothing has changed but the label.

This danger is increased when high school teachers are reluctant to teach in junior high schools. In many places, the junior high schools are therefore staffed by elementary school teachers and the approach to learning resembles the elementary schools' standards more than that of the high schools.

Here, then, is the classic example of the growing conflict, among teen-agers, between intellectual postponement and social speed-up.

The discrepancy is made even sharper by one additional complicating factor in value judgments: the question of competition. The proponents of education-without-pressures considered academic competition a hangover from the days of the regimented, authoritarian school: It makes children compare unequal talents. It leads to hurt feelings and to inferiority complexes. It offends the virtuous desire to teach pupils, above all else, "to learn to get along with each other."

All this is true if kept in perspective. Unfair or cutthroat competition is despicable, though widespread, in "real life." It is even more intolerable among children in school. The parents who, for example, are trying to force their children with an academic shoehorn into colleges with academic standards way beyond the unfortunate students' capacities, are doing infinite and lasting harm.

But real and reasonable competition is part of human motivation. As long as it has its place in life, adult or adolescent, it also has a rightful place in school. The surprising element in the attempt to eliminate competition from the schools is that those who tried so hard to make learning noncompetitive were the educational theorists most determined to make the schools a mirror of life.

Perhaps it was their devotion to the Utopian dream-society rather than the world of reality, perhaps it was their own insecurity and their own resulting fear of competition which made them rationalize that the only true competition for young minds is the contest of each individual with his own best potential.

Unfortunately, this theory assumes the impossible because it expects each person to live up to an uncomfortable ideal. It overlooks powerful nondriving forces: human inertia, self-satisfaction and laziness.

Even on those terms alone, the noncompetitive teen-ager would be doomed to performance way below his capacity. But two other troublesome factors enter the picture: first, that the same people who deplore intellectual competition frequently encourage physical or athletic competition; second, in the absence of competitive goals set for teen-agers by adult educational leadership, the so-called peer group will proclaim its own competitive tasks and tests.

What are the consequences?

Since healthy young people want to compete, their elders' implied warning against intellectual competition and tacit approval of physical competition channels their energies excessively into the battle of games rather than the battle of wits. This would not be so serious if physical competition could involve the great mass of teen-agers; but it does not. While everybody is a participant in the classroom, it is perfectly respectable to be in the bleachers during the athletic contest. Cheering, in fact, appears to be part of the competition and, as intricate training procedures and pep rallies have demonstrated, cheering can be a highly specialized part of this competitive activity.

A good yardstick for the confusion is the vehemence with which many educators condemn the excitement before some of the more decisive academic tests, such as the College Board Examinations, compared with the widespread acceptance of a determined and systematic whipping up of emotional frenzy before football or basketball games.

The peculiar double standard could not escape even the less sensitive teen-agers. Since getting into the "right" college is one of their more pressing concerns today, they could hardly be expected to overlook that "mere" superior academic performance will only render them equals among others with similar achievements, while outstanding athletic reputation places them in a preferred position of stardom.

In a recent year, when competition for admission to the "prestige" colleges was already frantic, one of these institutions frankly told a boy with a mediocre academic record but three varsity letters in high school that, if he applied no place else, he would be assured admission. The message could hardly be lost on his classmates.

John Ewing, a senior at Northport (N.Y.) High School, where he had been a member of a winning mathematics team, said that while his trophies from mathematics competitions had gained him some recognition among his fellow students, he felt that he was still far below a football or basketball player on the popularity list.

But he also offered a bright teen-ager's judgment concerning competition—a judgment quite different from that of many overly protective adults. "I like math and plan to teach it someday," he said. "But I don't think I would do this much research on its phases at this time if it weren't for the math fairs and competitions."

Alfred Kalfus, a mathematics teacher, agreed. "These brilliant youngsters need an outlet for their special energies just as much or more so than do the brawny ones," he said.

The only solution to this dilemma of double standards is in a sensible extension of the competitive idea to the important life of the mind. This solution is best described by Paul Woodring in his book *One Fourth of a Nation*. Just as it is absurd for a one-legged man to compete on the track with Roger Bannister, so it would be foolish to have students in the classroom compete with Albert Eistein—or to let outstanding students challenge on equal terms those of limited intelligence. But real contests of the mind among classmates as well as the admiration and respect for the really great minds, at least in equal measure with the hero worship of the gridiron stars, should be part of the development of teen-agers.

The doubts about academic competition and the condoning of athletic competition have reinforced among teen-agers a strong feeling that individual excellence is less acceptable than the winning team. This is a view which has its strong counterpart in modern American adult society, with its doubts about strong individual leadership and its substitute faith in committee effort.

Since adults have evolved the ideology of permissiveness, self-expression, and absence of competition, they find it harder to rechannel the energies of teen-agers, energies which have a natural edge of exuberance and endurance over those of the adults, into more mature directions. There even seems to be something of a parallel between the gradual abdication of the older society to the dictates of the younger and the anxiousness of the more experienced and more mature Western nations not to interfere with the often baffling, sometimes foolish and occasionally dangerous ways of the young and primitive underdeveloped nations. In both cases, the reluctance to exert influence, even where such influence would be sure to avert grief and suffering, is to an understandable extent based on the consciousness of past sins and mistakes.

The parallel does not stop there. Just as the more primitive underdeveloped nations, reveling in their unaccustomed independence, imitate the least desirable status-giving trappings of the older, more experienced countries, the independent and isolated teen-age society tends to pick the least valuable, indeed often the shabbiest aspects of the adult world.

A striking example of the tendency within the teen-age culture to absorb the most dubious standards of adult society is the apparently widespread acceptance among adolescents that girls ought to be intellectually inferior. This feeling is so strong that an overwhelming number of girls appear to be willing to be considered intellectually second-best. In his book, *The Adolescent Society,* James S. Coleman reports that in an upper-middle-class school not one of the girls "in the top leading crowd" said she wanted "to be remembered as a brilliant student."

In imitation of the lowest-common-denominator values of adult society, Mr. Coleman found that "the boy who is named as the best scholar does not want to think of himself as a brilliant student nearly so much as the best athlete wants to think of himself as an athletic star." But, he adds, "the boy scholar . . . is far more likely to want to see himself as a scholar than is the girl scholar who is presumably repelled by the culture's negative evaluation of this image. The lack of social reward for the girl who is thought of as best scholar makes it understandable that these girls, good students though they might be, would not flock to this image in great number."

How compelling the pressures of teen-age society can be is again documented when the Coleman study shows that over a four-year period the best girl students become strikingly less likely to want to be remembered for scholastic success, while the boys become more eager for it. "This examination of budding intellectualism in the high schools—and, as a cynic might put it, the way in which it can be nipped in the bud by the values of the adolescent culture—suggests the powerful impact that the adolescent culture can have on the larger society," Mr. Coleman concludes. "People who can and do achieve scholastically are a nation's intellectual resource; if the social system within which their education takes place undercuts any desire to think of themselves, and be thought of, as intellectuals, then these resources stand a good chance of being wasted or ill-used."

The danger of such waste, incidentally, is most serious in the middle- and upper-middle-class surroundings. (In working-class schools and families, apparently, the need and the desire for betterment still serves as a strong enough motive for scholastic effort to oppose the trend of waste through a reluctance to excel.) Among white-collar, middle-class girls, Mr. Coleman reports, "the 'activities girl'—the clubwoman of the high school—has pre-empted the place held by the outstanding girl scholar in the working-class schools."

The girl "clubwoman" is a strong influence within teenage society. Mr. Coleman sees this influence in terms of a shift from a passive role to active pace-setting. As the "activities girl" becomes a "Big Wheel" in the school, though not by reason of academic brilliance, she "responds less to the demands of parents, more to the demands of the adolescent community; she strives to be a leader in those activities the adolescent culture holds important rather than striving to achieve in what parents and teachers hold important."

Coleman's girl "clubwoman" has, of course, her male counterpart. Edgar Z. Friedenberg says in his book, *The Vanishing Adolescent*: "The big man on campus is a perfectly executed scale model of a junior executive." This is hardly surprising since "student life in the modern high school is now conducted through a veritable rat-maze of committees."

Mr. Coleman appears convinced that the long-range effect

of this kind of adolescent, isolated society (or societies) is harmful to adult America. He warns:

"The implications for American society as a whole are clear. Because high schools allow adolescent societies to divert energies into athletics, social activities, and the like, they recruit into adult intellectual activities many people with a rather mediocre level of ability, and fail to attract many with high levels of ability."

He quotes an articulate teen-ager: "As an adolescent, looking at our society from a distance, it seems to be merely an immature adult society. This immaturity is responsible for the 'world of difference' between the culture of the teen-ager and the adult. Immaturity and lack of responsibility lower the goals and standards of an adolescent society. The adolescent borrows for his society the 'glamourous and sophisticated' part of adult society. The high goals and worth-while activities of the adult world are scorned because they involve responsibilities, which the adolescent is not ready to accept."

Just as the underdeveloped country may, for reasons of glamour and status, squander millions on the operation of an impressive overseas airline, at the expense of building up even the most essential basic communications for its citizens in their day-to-day life, so the teen-age society tends to confuse the adult society's worst status-seeking and social climbing with real progress and achievement. The glamourous shambles of show business are more attractive than the hard labor of artistic endeavor. Slick-magazine "homemaking" is a more effective lure than normal housekeeping.

Anyone who criticizes teen-age standards runs into angry counterattacks by those who point out, quite accurately, that there are many serious young people, with admirable school records, great intellectual curiosity and high aspirations. These teen-agers, moreover, live fine and constructive lives and are not at all corrupted by the low standards of some of their contemporaries.

All this is true. The point is that these admirable teen-agers are resisting the teen-age society rather than leading it. They have set themselves apart, just as some adult intellectuals, despairing of influencing mass culture and its downward pull of gravity, have insulated themselves and their lives. This is preferable to a complete abdication to the forces of vulgar tastes and shoddy yardsticks; but it is not the way to turn the tide. And as the tide of society—in our instance that of the teen-age subculture—grows stronger, it requires correspondingly greater strength of character to resist it.

This is why an education system which, both in its way of life and in its way of learning, tends to be child-centered and adolescent-oriented (in contrast to the school designed for pupils by *adults,* as urged by Dr. Fischer), merely gives power to the tide of the adolescent subculture. Since the school is the major potential extension of adult influence into adolescent life, abdication by the school to teen-age standards builds an official moat around the fortress of teen-age isolation.

The effect is self-reinforcing. Parents who have gone through the adolescent-oriented school not only regard this as the normal, perhaps the only, way of bringing up their own children; they are also quick to lash out at other parents who disagree, as insensitive, selfish reactionaries. Thus, school and home become allies in isolating teen-age society and giving it jurisdictional powers over its mores and its education far beyond any teen-age Bill of Rights ever devised elsewhere.

The net results, says Mr. Coleman, is that "our adolescents today are cut off, probably more than ever before, from the adult society. They are still oriented toward fulfilling their parents' desires, but they look very much to their peers for approval as well. Consequently, our society has within its midst a set of small teen-age societies which focus teen-age interests and attitudes on things far removed from adult responsibilities, and which may develop standards that lead away from those goals established by the larger society."

One of the goals of society, often talked about and rarely pursued, is unfettered, rugged individualism. Its opposite—conformity—is being deplored almost around the clock, at P.T.A. meetings, at conferences of college presidents, in speeches for all occasions. It has been the subject of sociological studies, of novels such as *The Man in the Gray Flannel Suit,* and best-selling nonfiction books such as *The Organization Man.*

Many contributing factors are blamed for the growing threat of conformity and the increasing desire by even the more intelligent members of society to conform. The bigness of almost everything in our age, the size of corporations and the mushroom growth of towns, cities, and suburbs, undoubtedly push the individual toward the reassuring herd, with its shared anxieties and diminished personal responsibility. The importance of organizations, not only in the corporate field or in the labor unions but within the professional societies of doctors, lawyers, teachers and college professors as well, has made the passing of resolutions a more common-place road to action or excuse for inaction than the personal resolve for individual behavior and planning. Waiting for the consensus, or at any rate for majority judgment, by the "membership" is infinitely more soothing to the peace of mind than making a lonely decision. Presenting the findings of a consumer survey, a man-in-the-street public-opinion poll, a straw vote or a rating report is much less unsettling to the sales executive, the politician, the school administrator or the television program director than the risk of leadership.

Over all of it hangs the impersonal force of something that in the past may have been shrugged off as "fate," but has now become a man-made threat of uncertainty. Instead of the old forces of nature and the unknown "acts of God," today's preoccupation is with nuclear weapons and man-made, scientific dangers. Yet, even science itself has become Big Science and some scientists have turned themselves into Organization Men, subject to many of the same pressures of the team and the group as the leaders in industry.

These are among the reasons given whenever "conforming" among young people is deplored at panels and from rostrums.

None of this encourages individualism. But to counteract this trend the schools ought to be academically less permissive. Those who oppose a prescribed academic curriculum of basic studies often say that they do so because they want to encourage individuality and nonconformist independence among students. They believe that the best educational preventive medicine against conformity is to give the individual the widest possible choice in what he wishes to study and the freest rein as to what he wants to express, create, discover.

This is a fallacy on which not only teen-age crowd-culture but adult conformity as well have been built. It over-looks the most essential quality in every true nonconformist: the strength of his convictions that what he knows is solid. What he knows! This is the crucial phrase and the dividing line between nonconformists and crackpots, between strong minds and self-indulgent exhibitionists. Churchill could afford to be a nonconformist in politics and war, not because he had been taught self-expression but because he knew history, among other things. Einstein could disregard protocol and appear at a formal wedding wearing a stocking cap, not because he had been taught to do what he wished but because his knowledge and achievements had lifted him to the rare level at which men can fix their own standards of behavior.

Young people conform, especially in the naturally uncertain and vacillating years of adolescence—not because they have not been taught to be independent, but rather because they have not been taught enough of anything. It is their uncertainty, their lack of self-confidence, rather than any educational regimentation or molding of minds that makes them huddle among the "crowd" and hug the comforting anonymity of their "peers."

Here is the completed circle. The danger course begins in the child-centered grade school, with its excessive reliance on small committee-like groups. It is compounded when, in the interest of individual preferences, young pupils are permitted to postpone the acquisition of essential knowledge and adolescents are allowed, by selecting too much of their study menu, to leave painful voids in their intellectual progress.

Aware of those gaps, young people conform, just as their elders who are conscious of their weaknesses and insecurities bow to the dictates of their neighbors, their corporations or their organizations. The only reason why an Organization Man (adult) will remain silent when he thinks he ought to speak out is that he is not really sure of his ground—either the immediate ground of the argument at issue or the more important ground of his competence to do as well elsewhere, if he is fired.

These same defense mechanisms are at work among teenagers. They are unsure of their ground. The brightest among them are conscious of this deficiency. In his report on youth, Dr. George Gallup says that the most frequent complaint among high school students is about poor teachers: "They're not interested and they don't get us interested." These students complain, even today when college admission pressures have considerably tightened standards, that their education is "too easy." Dr. Gallup adds: "As a group they wish they had been forced to take more courses in foreign languages, literature, science, mathematics, history and philosophy."

Does this mean that these young people are against individual freedom and for regimentation, against self-expression and for the authoritarian school? Of course not. But they appear to understand more clearly than some of their educators that freedom and self-expression must be based on a store of knowledge and the security of experience.

In the early days of the liberal education reforms at the University of Chicago, the story goes, a student's father complained to the dean that he could not understand why undergraduates were told exactly what courses they had to take while they were permitted to be absent from classes and lectures as much as they pleased. He accused the University of being inconsistent. The dean replied that freedom is not an absolute commodity. To be free, an individual must understand the privileges he is given. An undergraduate, he concluded, could not possibly be expected to know what parts of the classics, which aspects of mathematics and what teachings of philosophy would turn out to be most essential to his liberal education—and so he needed the guiding hand of those who had read and experienced more than he. But this same student could be expected to be experienced and mature enough to know how important it is for him to be present in class. Hence, giving him freedom to determine his conduct was by no means inconsistent with the relative lack of freedom in selecting his courses.

In the absence of the security of knowledge, students substitute fads for more normal independent action. On the surface, these fads—from unconventional dress to obscure language—may appear to be the essence of nonconformity. In face, they are not; quite the contrary, they are conformity reduced to absurdity. For while the teen-age fads, often totally incomprehensible to the adult world, may seem distinguished by their daring difference from society, this is an illusion. Since teen-age society is a fortress unto itself, the fad within it is as solid in its conformity as the behavior of the most housebroken Organization Man in suburbia. These adolescent conformists have been trained in their own subculture to do the bidding of the group. They will emerge as the perfect replacements of their conforming elders.

The clue to the antidote should be plain from even a cursory look at teen-age society today. Who are the true nonconformists among this subculture? Not the "activity girls" or the cheerleaders, not the beatniks, conforming to shabby obscurantism, nor the hot-rodders. The nonconforming teen-agers are those with strong interests, those who have competed in the sciences and languages and the arts and, having built the foundation of self-confidence, have the strength to set their own pace and break out of the confinement of their peer-dominated subculture.

2 *Hothouse Bodies in a Cool Culture*

Early in her career of unsuccessful romances (while she was still in her teens) Elizabeth Taylor, the film actress, was reported to have complained that she had a child's mind in a woman's body. Hers is the classic definition of the teen-age dilemma.

Adults who have been away from the teen-age social scene for even a decade find to their surprise or, if they are parents of teen-agers, with a sense of shock that dating has become a junior high school and even elementary school activity. *The P.T.A. Magazine* says that "teachers in many communities across the nation report that some nine-year-olds are beginning to date and twelve-year-olds are going steady." Although these new patterns are not yet the rule in all parts of the country, the magazine predicts that "it seems likely that sooner or later this general trend will hit most communities."

"Dating" as a pairing of girls and boys may not be an American phenomenon as such; but as highly formalized, socially defined protocol it has become an American ritual that still makes foreign teen-agers on visits to the United States rub their eyes in disbelief. If anyone doubts the ritualistic aspects of the matter, Art Unger's *Datebook's Complete Guide to Dating* should set him straight. Its contents include carefully defined varieties of dates, to wit: First Dates, Double Dates, Dutch Dates, Meet-the-Family Dates, Church Dates, Study Dates, Prom Dates, Car Dates, Blind Dates, Dinner Dates, Stay-at-Home Dates, Spectator Sports Dates, Active Sports Dates, Concert Dates, and Museum Dates.

Dating as a ritual for high school youngsters and adolescents below that level has come into its own since World War II. Earlier, most activities were carried out in groups (partly to avoid the never very popular need for supervision by chaperone), and a young couple had to be determined, resourceful and adventurous to go off to "be alone together." For one thing, it was hard for them to find a place to go.

Now, they only need a car.

Two changes are important: the dating age is continuously getting younger; and dating is a social "must," the expected way of teen-age life. In fact, even the fears and anxieties connected with dating are accepted and welcomed as a sign of belonging. Less than a generation ago, a fifteen-year-old boy or girl "without a date" must have been privately unhappy, but he or she was nothing to worry about publicly. Today, the teen-ager who is not dating regularly at that age appears to be everybody's problem.

This social tyranny is the teen-age reflection of a society that has made a fetish of matchmaking and which considers it a hostess' duty to have a partner of the opposite sex for every "bachelor girl" or eligible male at every dinner party.

The American inquisition which subjects any unmarried young adult in his or her early twenties to immediate cross-examination—"Why aren't you married yet?"—is equally meddlesome in teen-age society. "Why aren't you dating?" might just as well mean "What's wrong with you?" Dr. Evelyn Millis Duvall in her book, *The Art of Dating,* says: "A girl who doesn't want to be too obvious in her datelessness may feign busyness or an intense interest in music or her family, for instance, to cover up for her lack of boy friends."

Cover up she must. But while this may get her over an immediate crisis, society must not let matters rest there. Dr. Duvall continues: "It's a good idea to investigate the reason why a particular individual is slow to get started dating. Is she shy and bashful? Then maybe she needs encouragement in getting social experiences; maybe he or she needs to be drawn into a group activity as a starter." The idea that a teen-age boy or girl might actually have a serious outside interest is not even considered as a possibility.

Another publication is even blunter. It urges parents to stop complaining about their teen-age children's early dating and tells such old-fashioned diehards that they "would do better to accept it gladly as one of the evidences of all-around healthy personality."

In short, the twosome approach to teen-age social life no longer is optional. In the *National Education Association Journal,* Dr. John J. Morgenstern, a school psychologist (who deplores the trend) tells of a pretty junior in high school who began to do badly in all her academic work around February. It turned out that she was in a state of long-range panic over the thought that she might not get a date for the Spring Dance in May. By April, rather than run the risk of remaining dateless and in disgrace, she accepted a date with a boy she did not like. Her misery, of course, was complete when a boy she did like finally asked her.

In another instance, girls in ninth grade voted to restrict the sale of tickets for a junior-high-school-leaving dance to couples only.

There is, of course, nothing wrong with dating as such. It is, or ought to be, the natural way for young people of the opposite sex to get to know each other. What is wrong about it today is the aura of frantic compulsion and the rushing of the season. Girls who have their "sweet sixteen parties" or, a few years later, their "coming out" debuts actually have been "out" for six years, and there is no longer any real occasion to be festive.

In line with the hothouse approach to making children grow up, summer resorts encourage parents to have their children, and certainly their teen-agers, attend night clubs until the early morning hours. Other resorts, carrying the trend a little further, advertise teen-age night clubs as a novelty. As a result of this stress on early "maturing," dating becomes a forced, not a natural activity for adolescents.

Margaret Mead, the anthropologist, said in an article for the Associated Press: "Instead of letting boys and girls go their separate ways, in late childhood and adolescence, we are forcing them to practice, not how to be individuals, but how to be spouses and parents; catapulting them into premature, half-baked adulthood before they have a chance to grow up as individuals."

A by-product of the early dating system is, of course, an unwarranted and often extreme financial pressure. A fourteen-year-old boy may spend in one evening a sum which it takes his father as many hours to earn—largely because "the other kids" spend as much and the most affluent of the "other kids" set the pace. A girl's proper party dress can become a major family crisis. In addition to the expenses of football games, club dues, special class functions, costumes for the school play and the many other extras, many parents know that they are expected to reciprocate for the increasingly expensive entertainment their teen-agers have been invited to in other homes. Everywhere the competition is on.

The Coke-and-hamburger date is in danger of becoming entirely the province of the ten-year-olds, who outgrow it when they hit the teens. By the time junior high school graduation comes around, they are used to much grander things, and the end of high school calls for really doing the town. It is no longer unusual for a teen couple in a big city to spend from $50 to $75 for that occasion. (It might be added that spending an equal amount for a year's supply of college textbooks is decried as a shameful indication of the high cost of learning by most parents.)

Reuel Denney, co-author of *The Lonely Crowd*, wrote in *Daedalus:* "The high school student of today has taken up the ceremonial burden of graduating in a manner befitting the college graduate of earlier years. He expects to be equipped with cars, white jackets, carnations, orders for corsages, and all the other equipment of role and status that in my day as a stripling were reserved by the Florist's Association, the Cadillac ads, the pages of *Vanity Fair,* and the apparel shops for well-off adults and a small number of country club sprouts."

Closely linked with the cost of early dating and the effects of affluence is the stress on popularity. Carlfred B. Broderick, professor of family relationships at Pennsylvania State University, writes in *The P.T.A. Magazine* that "early daters are among the most popular children in their schools—popular with their own as well as the opposite sex." But while the judgment of their immature peers is understandable, that of their teachers is inexcusable. Yet, the same source tells us that "teachers tend to rate them above average in social maturity." This is a little like rating successful embezzlers as above average in fiscal maturity.

The heartbreak that can be the consequence of the all-important quest for popularity is described in a letter from a teen-ager to *Teen Magazine.* It tells of the price paid for being a "socie"—a socially prominent—*i.e.,* popular—member of the teen-age set. She wrote in part:

"Every boy or girl who attends high school knows the definition of 'socie.' If they aren't classified as one, they learn how to put up with them and like it!

"I became a socie this year. When I first entered high school, I was an average teen-age girl. . . . Then I tried out for and made majorette. It was not by means of popularity, but by knowledge of baton-twirling that I won this title. Boy, did spectacular things start happening to me! I was now in the limelight, along with all 'those' kids.

"Because of my being on Pep Squad and a leader of the school, my life drastically changed.... All it takes is to be seen with the top kids or be included with them as I was through Pep Squad. I found myself without enough days for all the dates.... Now that I have been 'discovered' all sorts of wonderful things began happening. My most impressive accomplishment was being chosen Lettermen Queen in the Junior year.... [But] it was just because all the other girls on Pep Squad had been exhausted because they had been 'used' for other Queens and I was the lucky newcomer to be chosen next.... The popular kids aren't what they want you to believe.... Think twice before you long to become a socie."

Popularity has become the big prize and an obsession. Children compete for it desperately and, often egged on by their parents, are ready to buy it, if their personal assets appear insufficient guarantee for popularity success. To prove the parents' part in the rat race for popularity, Dr. Morgenstern reports that many private dance studios cater to parents who want their nine-year-olds to "be ready for junior high school and not left out." He quotes an elementary school principal: "All this should be postponed until the eighth and ninth grade but I want my kids to be able to compete in junior high with those from wealthier homes who've had private dancing lessons."

Social or dancing "readiness" has become as important as reading readiness was once thought to be. What might be called the Cult of Popularity has become the key to teen-age behavior. The obsession with being "well-liked," dramatized with such desperate urgency as the great American adult sickness, has become the overriding teen-age motivation. Just as the tragedy *Death of a Salesman* made the important distinction between merely "being liked" and "being well-liked," teen-agers in suburbia classify classmates as being "popular," "medium popular" or "very popular," with many shadings in between. This search for popularity does not permit much room for individualism or independent thought and action.

Sociologist James Coleman in his study of teen-agers finds that while academic success has some bearing on the popularity of boys among boys and girls among girls, the major popularity factors among teen-agers of the opposite sex are clothes for girls and cars for boys. Thus, the stress on both co-education and dating in today's school society distorts the entire value system. Unless a girl chooses to be a model or an actress, clothes and external beauty will never again be as important to her as they appear to be during the high school years. "The adult women in whom such attributes are most important are of a different order from wives, citizens, mothers," Coleman concludes. "They are chorus girls, models, movie and television actresses and call girls. In all these activities women serve as objects of attention for men and even more, objects to attract men's attention. . . . If the adult society wants high schools to inculcate the attributes that make girls objects of attracting men's attention, then these values of good looks and nice clothes are just right."

There is, of course, nothing new about the desire of fourteen-year-old girls to be models or movie stars. But with the impact of the mass media, the availability of "grown-up" beauty aids and the lack of adult intervention when adolescent daydreaming is translated into daily action and "normal" behavior, the fantasy emerges as a way of life. All of this is scrambled into an unhealthy omelet of shallow appearances and hazily comprehended sex, often mistaken for love. Coleman points out, for example, that in response to his question, "What are the best things that might happen to me in school this year?" all the girls' answers were related to boys, dating and popularity.

Apologists for early maturing have made a strong point of saying that concern for "grooming" and "life-adjustment" is good experience for adult life. The inherent fallacy is the disregard for the damage that can be done by misplaced or excessive emphasis. This is comparable to the standard argument of the typical football coach at the alumni dinner, holding forth about the body- and character-building quality of the gridiron. The trouble is that varsity football prepares none of the players (except the occasional star who turns pro) for anything that can be applied to "real life"—not even to regular sports and physical exercise. By the same yardstick, the new teen-age cults of popularity, personality and glamour-grooming—especially since they are usually divorced from all standards of discriminating taste—prepare for no worth-while adult "life adjustment."

If the main stress were to be on neatness and attractive appearance, all the concern for grooming would, of course, be highly commendable. But far too much of the glamour-seeking, in the absence of adult limits, depends on excessive expenditures. What, then, happens to the girl who is not expensively dressed, glamorously groomed and physically well-endowed? She is faced with the curse of not being popular. Feeling "left out" and rejected in a culture which puts so much stress on being dated becomes a serious matter which, according to many psychologists' testimony, may injure permanently a girl's view of herself as a woman. That this danger is not seriously recognized can be deduced from high school courses which make "personality" development part of the curriculum. Often the "academic" aim of such teaching is defined as becoming "datable" or "lovable." By the same token, the boy who fails to impress girls with his athletic prowess and, in addition, lacks spending money and a car cannot help but begin to see himself as a failure as a "man."

Even those who, by teen-age standards, are "successful" are hurt by the frantic pace of popularity. For them, the highly organized and formalized dating ritual and the fickle rating system requires constant vigilance. Phone calls, planning, arrangements, protocol, shopping for clothes and cosmetics leave insufficient time for the development of other interests. It is quite the rule today to hear parents complain about the academic pressures on their youngsters. And while excessive competition for grades and college admission can be harmful, in many instances the pressures become excessive only because teen-agers refuse to realign their priorities. If the more rigorous educational demands are to be added to an unchanged schedule of dating, preoccupation with cars, fan clubs and other social activities, then the total strain becomes unbearable. This is hardly the way to approach life, even in adolescence.

Moreover, schoolwork still proceeds at a relatively regulated pace, sometimes close to lock step, while all speed limits have been removed from social and, in many instances, sexual progress. Even without such latitude, adolescence is a confusing time, with new interests and only half-understood feelings and emotions pulling in many, often opposite, directions. With the addition of group pressures, encouraged by some parents and much of the advice literature, the confusion is compounded. At first, the earlier "social activities" were to serve as training ground for "the real thing." The dating youngsters in school, so the theory went, were to learn to feel comfortable and self-reliant in the company of the opposite sex. Thus, the high school girl would arrive poised and sophisticated on the college campus once she had the independent role of a co-ed to play.

In practice, things work differently. Dating and the prelude to advanced social activities cannot be put in the same category as a College Board aptitude test for which you may take a set of preliminaries which "don't count." Youngsters consider all their social activites "real," rather than trial runs. It would be foolish to expect them to feel differently. The danger comes when social activity outruns mental, rational, intellectual and ethical development.

One of the most telling definitions of education is that it must teach the ability of considering the consequences of one's actions. To expect teen-agers to have this ability is absurd; to let them behave as though they had it is playing with fire. Some of this intellectual maturing may begin in the upper years of high school, but it does not, for most adolescents, come during the teens—certainly not before college age. This is why it is particularly dangerous to transfer college mores into the lower schools.

To be completely fair to the teen-agers themselves modern American living has not been of much help to them. Lack of space and the decline of privacy, even in relatively well-to-do homes, has driven young people toward the only convenient avenue of escape: living in their own groups. Whether they are brought up in crowded city apartments or in suburban homes (ranch-style or split-level), there is little room for them to turn inward. A two-car garage today appears more important than a separate dining room, thus giving the automobile greater privacy than its owners. The cult of togetherness, shrewdly encouraged by space-saving architects, has created the "family room" as a jumbled combination of living room, dining "area," kitchen, study, library and play room. Perhaps, in modern America, time is no longer money, but space is. The resulting lack of space has deprived too many adolescents of that important chance to sulk or dream—alone.

One more reason for the crowd to take over!

The result of all this is not only simulated "adult" social life during the years of adolescence; it is also the establishment of a highly formalized protocol which puts additional pressure on those teen-agers who would prefer not to conform. Because of the great importance of popularity, for example, and the fear of being without a date and left out, "going steady" has become a kind of "social security" for teen-agers. It has many of the implications of the old betrothal or engagement, but none of the justification. Where the period of engagement serves an important psychological prelude to marriage, going steady merely eliminates competition in young people's social contacts. Thus, ironically, it defeats even the purpose of those who saw in early dating a process of learning and a sharpening of judgment. Instead of permitting teen-agers to sharpen their wits, test their emotions and extend their knowledge of people, the monogamous dating ritual limits horizons and makes the eventual decision of selecting a marriage partner even more hazardous than it has ever been. Incidentally, the traditional double standard works against the girls' interests even in this latest form of pairing off: Dr. Gallup's survey found that more girls reported that they were going steady than did boys. The most likely reason, Dr. Gallup suggested, is that the girls think they are going steady, while the boys may not tell the full story of their extra-steady-dating relationships.

It is never easy to translate trends and habits into statistics. The Gallup survey concluded that young people overwhelmingly approve of the idea of going steady, but that only about 20 per cent actually do it. Both boys and girls agree that it is socially safer and less nerve-wracking to go steady. Boys say that if they steady-date a girl, they know what she wants and therefore feel more comfortable. They don't need to get up their courage to ask for a date and are spared the humiliation of a rejection. They even feel that, in the long run, it is cheaper since it eliminates repetition of that most expensive initial period of "impressing a date."

Girls, too, value the knowledge that they can count on having a date, especially since this increasingly is the admission ticket to all social functions of importance.

Some parents go along with the trend and believe that the security of knowing with whom their children are more or less "paired off" reduces their worries.

The impact of steady dating makes young lives less youthful. It molds them to the image of "married security." It reduces competition and imposes "old" habit, without the benefit of proper preparation or the excitement of growing up.

The ritual is fairly well defined, although there are variations from community to community. In many places, where the going-steady custom is well established, a girl or boy only needs to date the same person three or four times in a row. Competitors will then stay away and leave the two in teen-age union.

All such arrangements are not, of course, necessarily the result of overwhelming personal feelings. Often prestige plays an important part. The captain of the football team, who understandably looks for the prettiest girl in the senior class, is a prize to be carried off. Unfortunately, since "prestige couples" tend to be in the limelight, the pressure on them to make their relationship serious and permanent becomes even stronger. It needs hardly be said that this kind of "union" rarely has the stuff of which reliable and compatible marriages are made.

Steady dating has been damned and praised by teen-agers, parents and "experts." It has been eulogized as the answer to the promiscuity of earlier generations and decried as a new kind of immorality. The important point is that, whether good or bad in itself, it has transferred the problems and anxieties in the relationship between the sexes from the college age-group to the high school and even the junior high school. This is why any comparison with the dating habits of earlier generations is misleading. It may be perfectly justifiable to criticize the actions and the morals of the "Flaming Youth" of the twenties—but these were not the actions and morals of teen-agers. F. Scott Fitzgerald was anything but a moralist or prude, but he might very well be startled by the standards and actions of teen-agers today. His young men and women did a good deal of "unconventional" experimenting. Many of them never grew up and let their foolishness run them aground. But there may be even more serious danger in the modern teen-ager's drift toward "settling" early for security.

The real problem is the teen-ager's transition from immature, group-organized "social security" to the inevitable excitement of sexual feelings, both real and dictated by adolescent and adult-playing society.

3 *Sex: Little Old Technicians*

A suburban high school principal, asked at a dinner party what was his students' most serious single problem, replied without a moment's hesitation: "Sex."

Glamourous, exciting, daring, bare-bosomed or intriguing, clinically frank or insinuatingly hinted at—sex is omnipresent. It must appear to teen-agers, raised in modern America, as the only yardstick of manhood and femininity. It is linked with the hero-symbols in society and Hollywood. It pervades the cosmetics advertising and the come-ons for attire, from foundations to accessories. Yet, this same age and culture, which fairly saturates the air and the air waves with the glossiest of sex worship, manages to produce adults who propose to protect high school seniors from the corrupting influence of a textbook account of the chaste practice of "bundling" in the Puritan past.

Contradictions abound. From early childhood, youngsters are permitted a wide range of curiosity and exploration. They are told that to express themselves freely, even on topics of which they are ignorant, is part of their educational birthright. They are encouraged to put self-expression ahead of self-discipline. They are given to understand that they must learn by experimentation rather than through the transmitted experience of their elders. Then—suddenly—they are expected to apply judgment and self-control to their emerging interest in sex—the area of human behavior in which even adults find it most difficult to practice wisdom and self-discipline.

Laurence Wylie, the sociologist, writes in *Daedalus:* "At church and school and home both boys and girls are told that it is wrong to express themselves sexually outside of wedlock. But walking home from school, in locker rooms, at the corner drugstore, from newspaper stories, from movies and magazines and TV, they learn that ideal standards are false. The American adolescent must choose between observing the standards and feeling frustrated and cheated, or violating the standards, feeling guilt and risking social sanctions."

Early "knowledge" without judgment and intellectual capacity enormously complicates the problem. Recently, a book was published for seven-year-olds in elementary school, explaining to them in full detail and with extensive illustrations the "problem" of sex. The theory, of course, is that knowledge is always better than ignorance and that an early, natural and educational approach will lead to understanding. Understanding, it is thought to follow, will lead to proper behavior.

This theory overlooks the importance of timing in the process of education. Even though the book offers "the story of conception, prenatal development and birth as children should learn it—and can understand it," the question remains whether any purpose is served by teaching children something that ought to remain outside of their experience for a long time.

Whether the story is true or apocryphal, the fallacy of assuming a child's early "need" to know about sex is effectively parodied by the mother's frantic attempt to answer in full detail her little grade school son's question: "Where did I come from?" After she had finished describing intercourse, insemination and conception with clinical accuracy, she was puzzled by the little boy's still doubtful, frowning look.

"Don't you understand what Mummie explained to you?" she asked.

"I understand what you told me," said the little boy. "But what I want to know is where I came from. Pete in my class said that he came from St. Louis. Where do I come from?"

The idea that, if children can be made to understand how dogs or birds or human babies are conceived, they will also comprehend the deeper meaning of reproduction and love, is both educational and scientific nonsense. The end result is that they look on sex as either a biological "function" or, if they believe the magazines, as story-book romanticism. Neither is sound, healthy or productive of a mature attitude toward either sex or love.

This applies equally to the practice of earlier dating. If a girl starts dating regularly at thirteen, the meaningful excitement she ought to feel about going out with boys when she is sixteen will become transferred to the frontiers of sexual exploration. From then on, marriage begins to beckon as nothing quite so much as a safe harbor.

Looking forward to "teen-age" has become a time consuming (and expensive) "pre-teen" pastime. *Time* magazine reports that an eight-year-old girl "needed" a garter belt and nylons for a party because "all the other girls" had them and that a nine-year-old girl asked her parents for a "training" bra to wear on a movie date with her eleven-year-old boy friend. In some of the wealthier suburbs, boys of ten are given formal co-ed, sit-down dinner dances. The pre-teens are now preparing for the "big" time by dating, dancing and playing kissing games.

"Many parents appear to operate under the mistaken theory that sex starts at puberty," says Carlfred B. Broderick of Pennsylvania State University, a professor of family relationships. "They assume that early kissing is meaningless. But pre-teen dating starts the youngster earlier on the road to progressive intimacy."

A Pittsburgh schoolteacher adds: "Some modern parents seem to feel that if their daughters don't begin to date in grade school, this indicates a lack of feminine appeal. They're afraid that their daughters will grow up to be old maids."

As for the boys, a Denver psychiatrist feels they are "seduced away from their normal lives. At an age when the boy should be going through the badly needed period of competitive play with other boys and teasing girls when he notices them at all, he finds himself pushed into a relationship with which he cannot cope."

A combination of co-education and premature social pressures creates an unreal atmosphere. Instead of permitting youngsters to grow up in an unselfconsciously carefree way—something co-education was originally meant to achieve—boys and girls even in their pre-teen years are made to be aware of differences they fail to understand. Rather than letting them go their separate ways, the pairing process is actually pushed, in the absence of a natural desire for it. This is aggravated by the uneven development of boys and girls, with the latter generally several years ahead in maturity, at least until boys catch up in the very late teens or early twenties.

At the awkward age, when boys and girls used to follow their natural instincts and avoid each other, except for occasional name-calling, they are now thrown together in a way that is meaningless, if not actually repulsive to them.

This encourages them to ape the behavior of older children or adolescents, almost in self-defense and to protect their sense of dignity. At an age when boys would much rather be off digging for worms or looking for tadpoles, they are made to act as though infancy had become the age of chivalry. Our adolescent, pair-conscious culture has forced boys and girls to pay attention to each other. Heaven help the modern eleven- or twelve-year-old (or even younger) boy who does not like girls. His parents are likely to stay up nights wondering whether they should consult with the guidance counselor or visit a psychiatrist. In the majority of instances, this will not be necessary: subtle pressures plus the reinforcement of group action will make the majority of youngsters do their bit to act as they are expected to.

Documenting the problem and the disagreement between generations is a letter from a worried grandmother to columnist Dr. Rose N. Franzblau: "My granddaughter, fifteen, is very pretty and most personable. At school she met a boy the same age and has been going steady with him for about six months. They are enamored of each other to the point that when you speak to them about breaking up, they practically melt into tears. My daughter has actually been enjoying the romance between the two children. At first she thought it was very cute, and said it would not get serious. But, of course, it has gotten serious. We keep telling my daughter that the girl is too young and they, the parents, should not let the youngsters see each other so much. But her parents sanction everything she does and they won't listen to us . . ."

It would, of course, be foolish to set specific age limits for one kind of interest or behavior and another. Children mature at different times and, as Margaret Mead put it, it should be up to each boy and girl to grow from one stage into another. That this is not the way "growing up" comes about today can best be seen from the revolution in the use of cosmetics. Lipstick illustrates the point. Back in grandma's day, lipstick was "shocking" as a general principle, the mark of painted and tainted women. In the twenties and thirties, lipstick was acceptable for grown young women, but not for teen-agers. Today, however, a study at the University of California, which compared adolescents of the thirties and the fifties, found that more ninth-graders (fourteen-year-olds) approve of the use of lipstick than eleventh-graders (seventeen-year-olds) did twenty years ago. And Dr. Mary Cover Jones, professor of education, who undertook the study, said that "lipstick symbolizes as well as any specific item could the sensitization in early adolescence toward being grown-up."

But events are already outrunning the sociological surveys. Lipstick, now fully accepted, is beginning to be considered old-hat. Eye-shadow has become a more important adult sex symbol. If the present trend continues, lipstick may be expected to move down from the upper elementary grades into kindergarten.

Of course, these are only the surface symptoms of more important, deeper problems. Girls may initially suffer most from this speed-up. They are pushed into the market place and have to compete earlier, and they have fewer commodities to offer in the popularity game than the boys. Mothers are torn between the desire to push their daughters into the popularity stream and the wish to protect them from being caught without control in the current. Cole Porter summed it up with, "It is he who has the fun and thee the baby." No amount of detached reason changes that basic truth.

Before the age of dating (and one hesitates to set any age limit for it today) girls may play kissing games, without concern about their reputations or involvement. But as soon as dating begins she faces the "how-far-should-I-go" question—and its bearing not only on her natural desires but on that compelling issue, popularity. In order to be in good standing, both with the girls and the boys, she must also preserve her reputation. In spite of the liberal approach to boy-girl relationships, Coleman reports that "the girl who is too free with herself, whatever her social background, is excluded—evidently first by the girls, with the boys concurring."

All of this leads with predictable and almost comic regularity to the same question in all the different advice columns and books. As a classic example, the question in Art Unger's book will serve as well as any:

"I like to kiss and neck. After I've gone out with a boy a few times, I don't think it's so wrong. But that doesn't mean I want to go all the way or anything like that. Yet this boy I used to see last month tried to go so much farther than I think is right. It happened while we were at a drive-in movie and we were necking. I told him No, but he insisted on trying. Why don't boys know enough to stop?"

Perhaps the most straightforward answer to this age-old question would be that any girl (or child) who does not know the answer should have stayed home. But since this answer would hardly be acceptable to the adolescent set, the social and educational machinery has ground out a whole series of protocols, rules and standard operating procedures. This is the typical contemporary American approach to all socio-ethical problems: instead of admitting that surface symptoms are the results of more basic causes, society laboriously pens a manual. This is done for the teaching of "moral and spiritual values" or so intangible a concept as "citizenship" in the schools; it is done by way of a "code" in various professions. Why not for the relationships between teen-age boys and girls?

A girl uses her appearance, her charm or her "favors" as currency to bargain for desirable dates which, in turn, are legal tender in the exchange of popularity. According to the rules, a certain number of dates, rate a kiss. The standard question in the advice books is: "Should I let him kiss me good-night on our first date?" Most books answer in the negative, but leave leeway for exceptions. A standard caution in teen-age advice literature is that, if the boy "gets" his kiss on the first date, he may assume that many other boys have been just as easily compensated. In other words, the rule book advises mainly that the popularity assets should be protected against deflation. Such considerations as maturity, ethics, affection, love (or even passion and infatuation) do not enter the picture; it turns almost entirely on the rational, if not outright commercial, consideration of popularity purchase.

This rule-book approach might be thought comic, were it not so desperately empty and devoid of emotional warmth and social maturity. Dr. Duvall, for example, reports that a girl told her: "She is expected to give a good-night kiss on the first date, to neck on the second date, pet on the third, and then she has to fight for her honor the fourth time she is out with the fellow."

And nothing could illustrate blind faith in rule-book answers more devastatingly than a letter to columnist Ann Landers: "How can I make a very good-looking guy keep his hands to himself? I like him a lot and don't want to lose him, but he's been getting out of line lately. Please hurry your answer. I have to know by Saturday night . . ."

David Riesman, co-author of *The Lonely Crowd,* calls sex "the last frontier" of privacy, and the younger the explorers cross the frontier, the more meaningless their group discussion of their exploits. "Dating at twelve and thirteen," writes Riesman, "the child is early made aware of the fact that his taste in emotions as well as in consumer goods must be socialized and available for small talk."

While early dating places unreasonable pressures on girls, it also creates an adolescent or pre-adolescent society in which boys are, at least socially, under the girls' domination. This is particularly true since, as has been pointed out already, girls are, at equal age, socially and biologically far more mature than boys. This junior matriarchy reinforces the relative absence of male leadership in a child's world today: fathers are busy and teachers are largely women, at least up to high school. In the suburbs, where most men commute and are absent from dawn to dinner (often past the children's bedtime), men are almost completely missing in the weekday routine.

The only remaining male preserve in adolescent society is the sports arena. But the effect of masculine strength there is limited to a small aristocracy. This is the world of the "natural athlete," the star. In a society which has made a national hero of the athlete, to the point of having the cream of our colleges bid against each other for his purchase, it is not surprising that he rules supreme in his own adolescent kingdom. He is a kind of "king bee," and he is automatically popular. He even has his squealing, professional, adolescent dancing girls—the cheerleaders—attending to his glorification on ceremonial occasions. Since adult college alumni and even deans of admission conspire to give this small group of adolescents the special privileges of an elite, it would be unreasonable to expect teen-agers themselves not to be equally impressed.

The trouble with the athletic aristocracy is that it is so small. Most teen-age boys never make the team or even the bench. The best they can hope for is to be accepted by those who count and to gain status by riding on such coattails of virility. The only other symbols that will gain them status and popularity are such possessions as cars, which in turn may lead to a favorable reputation among the more desirable girls. But while the athlete's popularity is automatic, that of ordinary mortals must be acquired, usually by submission to the girls' domination. Even if the boys, as is usually the case with the younger ones, would rather follow their more natural pursuits, the early-dating society has made girls, not unlike cars, a symbol of status and popularity.

David Riesman underlines this, when he says in *The Lonely Crowd:* "In male bull sessions, one can no longer play the gentleman and keep quiet sexual adventures. He has to furnish names, dates, and all the exact details of his conquest. Where fellows get into trouble is when they have a sincere feeling for a girl and yet are forced to tell."

But as the only vaguely understood social and sexual relationships of early dating and status-seeking romance become more important for popularity and prestige, the girls are as concerned about their conquests as the boys appear to be in their locker room talk. A reflection of this is the story of *Gidget Goes Hawaiian,* teen-age translated into fiction. The heroine and her rival try to give each other the impression that they have "gone all the way" with their adolescent boy friends, when actually they have not. In real life, teen-agers from one well-to-do Long Island community report that a girl is supposed to begin having sexual intercourse with her steady boy friend on the magical date of her sixteenth birthday—or lose status.

That this sixteen-year limit is only a tentative one for many teen-agers, and one likely to be pushed downward by the "mature" members of the crowd, goes without saying. One of the eleven anonymous Princeton seniors who speak about *The Unsilent Generation* in a book by that name, edited by instructor Otto Butz, looks back on his first full-fledged love affair. Both he and the girl, child of a well-to-do suburban upper-middle-class family, were sixteen at the time. About five years later, long after the first experiment in love and passion had faded away, he reminisced: "We were perfectly adjusted sexually, though in retrospect, I believe she was somewhat more experienced than I."

Quite aside from other questions of wisdom and morality, this trend further deprives the young male of the challenge of conquest: if teen-age mores make it part of the rule for the girl, at a certain chronological point, to part with her virginity, he becomes merely an agent in an already girl-dominated society.

Adult observers who want to put the stamp of approval on current trends make much of the fact that the new morality—early dating, going steady and natural drift into sexual contact and intercourse—is preferable to the old idea of boys getting their first initiation from "experienced older women," amateur or professional. The flaw in this comparison is, first, that once again the experimenting young male of earlier days (even of the period of Flaming Youth) was usually of college age. Second, today's teen-ager and his girl friend merely compound their own confusion, fears and inexperience, and neither gets any pleasure from the hasty and furtive act.

Coleman puts it this way: "More traditionally in adolescence, and still so among working-class boys, the relevant dichotomy is the good girl versus the bad girl—the first to respect and admire, the second to exploit and have fun with. It appears that this dichotomy is being replaced, in the modern middle class, with that of the active girl versus the passive girl—the first to respect and have fun with, the second to ignore."

Psychiatrist Bruno Bettelheim is more specific. In an article, "The Problem of Generations," which appeared in *Daedalus,* he writes: "American middle-class youth learns about sex in the back seat of a car, or during a slightly drunken party, or because there was nothing better to do to kill boredom. . . . The first sexual experience often leaves ineffaceable impressions, marred by a total lack of experience on either side. Both partners feeling anxious and insecure, neither one can offer encouragement to the other, nor can they take comfort from the accomplished sex act, since they cannot be sure they did it well, all comparisons lacking."

Probably as a result of their subconscious realization of all this, teen-agers have tried to solve some aspects of the dilemma by what might be called legalized petting, often interpreted as sexual intercourse without the final step, or less kindly referred to as "mutual masturbation." It is a "compromise" which permits a girl to retain technical virginity, to avoid pregnancy but to have sexual gratification nevertheless. This is, of course, a false assumption which highlights the limitations of the immature with their pathetic faith in techniques. It might even be traced back to the mistaken belief that sex and love can be defined entirely in terms of physical body functions. But satisfaction without love is as much a contradiction as religion without faith. Margaret Mead has described petting as a cooperative invention designed to cheat sex.

Whatever the definitions and rationalizations, there is general agreement that the old barriers and standards have vanished and that the few remaining ones are fast crumbling. Dr. David Mace, Executive Director of the American Association of Marriage Counselors, said in a *McCall's* article: "I have noticed, during the past ten years, a marked change on the part of student groups to the subject of premarital sex relations. They used to ply the visiting lecturer with questions on this topic. Nowadays such questions seldom come up. The subject is old hat. In high school groups, the girls often complain that nowadays the boys insist that if there is to be no petting, there will be no second date. In college groups, the students seldom parry questions about their sexual behavior. They admit frankly that many of them are having sexual intercourse."

David Boroff wrote in *Esquire* magazine: "Attitudes towards sex among those who grew up after World War II—those under thirty in other words—are strikingly different from other generations. . . . It can be summed up in this way: Sex is one of life's principal goods. . . . The loss of chastity is no longer the fall from innocence; it is the fall upward, so to speak, to maturity and self-fulfillment." As a consequence, a teen-ager today is more likely to feel that inexperience is unattractive and a demerit.

All this has not solved the basic problem, summed up bluntly by Ann Landers, that "girls get pregnant." Forty per cent of all babies born out of wedlock in this country are born to mothers nineteen years old or younger, according to the Children's Bureau of the Department of Health, Education and Welfare. (These statistics obviously fail to take into account the many more who, after they became pregnant, rushed into marriage, nor those who got rid of their babies through abortion.)

In New York City, the approximate annual registry of illegitimate births, recorded by the Department of Health, is 13,500, and 1,100 of the mothers are under eighteen. In Washington, D.C., one out of every five babies is born illegitimately, and a large percentage is born to teen-agers. A 1961 study by the Chicago Board of Education showed that 576 girls, all under sixteen and one as young as eleven, dropped out of school because they were pregnant. The *New York Times* reported that Dr. Margaret L. Cormack found that premarital pregnancy, "once a college problem, is now a high school and junior high school problem." She cited an estimated 240 pregnancies in one large New York junior high school in one year.

It is customary and comforting to blame slum conditions and broken homes for these early pregnancies. But while such conditions do inflate the statistics, they no longer can be used honestly to sweep the real problem out of sight of publicity. Many of the teen-age pregnancies are now reported, though frequently kept from public view, by wealthy, prosperous, middle-class homes. The most important percentage increase of premarital pregnancies has occurred in white, middle-class families. The unwed mother is no longer just the unfortunate, illiterate girl from the wrong side of the tracks, so long immortalized in American fiction and movies; she is just as likely to be the girl next door in a well-to-do suburb. One of New York City's voluntary hospitals on the wealthy East Side, from where it draws most of its clientele, reports that the single-girl confinement in the maternity section has jumped 271 per cent in six years.

Parents in a Connecticut suburb recently debated the problem with a mixture of shock and embarrassment. The issue never was tackled head-on. In fact, the most important question under discussion was whether to discuss it at all. The problem remained.

In the spring of 1961, eight girls of a senior high school class of forty boys and girls in a Long Island community were pregnant before graduation. Of these, six were planning marriage soon, one was determined not to marry, and the eighth girl was undecided. The last two plan to return to school when the infants are old enough to be left with the grandparents. An investigation of the pattern in that community showed the accepted convention, referred to earlier, to be one of sexual intercourse with one's steady boy friend at age sixteen. In two cases the teen-agers violated their own unwritten new conventions and began intercourse much sooner. This pattern was accompanied by heavy drinking, late hours and uninhibited parties, plus a cavalier attitude by the community.

These facts are no more than the bare skeleton of shifting teen-age sex attitudes. Pregnancies in themselves, it must be remembered, tell only a fraction of the story, particularly since knowledge about and access to contraceptives are more readily available than ever. (It should not be overlooked that the venereal disease rate among juveniles has been increasing seriously, despite greater availability of facts. And while it has become customary to attribute this increase entirely to the "usual" slums and broken homes, a study by New York City's Department of Health, conducted by Dr. Celia S. Deschin, shows that the majority of teen-agers with venereal diseases "did not come from impoverished or transient families" and had, in fact, enjoyed "fairly stable family lives." Only a minute minority, to spike another smug alibi, were Puerto Rican.)

Why is this happening? Why have adults—parents, teachers and other mature authorities and advisers—been unable to play a more active part in curbing what, even to the most permissive, must appear as sexual excesses?

The answer lies in the defeatism common to all areas of society's changing mores and in the acceptance of whatever exists at the moment as "normal." This acceptance is often blind enough to make people deny that what used to be might possibly have been preferable. In this spirit, Lillian Bye, executive director of Boston's Crittenton Hastings House (a home for unwed mothers), suggested at a national social welfare conference that, as the number of unwed mothers are increasing so rapidly, the unmarried and pregnant girl might in the future be considered "the established American woman who accepts conscious responsibility for her final freedom in sex and consequently for motherhood when it occurs, in or out of wedlock."

Whatever the future may hold, most parents today are not ready to accept so "liberal" a view. They are more likely to search for an explanation of what has been happening——in the hope of turning the tide. Much of the story is directly linked to the confusion between freedom and license, between self-expression and maturing, between growing up unguided and being educated through adult authority toward the eventual achievement of self-discipline.

The abdication of adult authority in other areas of bringing up young children has inevitably meant that the adolescents themselves rush to fill the vacuum. So it is with sex, too. Earlier knowledge of the facts, however incompletely understood, could not help but lead to earlier "experimentation," especially when experimentation per se had been made the supreme educational ideal. Finally, there was the understandable but often overindulgent desire to provide children with "everything"—even if this included the freedoms and facilities to make temptation irresistible for too many teen-agers weaned on early social and postponed intellectual maturity.

Time and again, parents admit that they disapprove of their children's freedom to come and go as they please. In too many instances (happily not in all, by any means) they also say that they are reluctant to be stricter than the parents of their children's friends. They are afraid of being considered prudes or old-fashioned, especially if the parents of other youngsters are socially or economically prominent. Frequently, a few "courageous" and intelligently outspoken telephone calls might lead to the discovery that other parents are beset by similar doubts. But such telephone calls are rarely made, and in their absence everybody tends to live up to the Joneses' imagined broadmindedness. (Of course, some parents "go it alone" in setting their rules, but neither they nor their children have much influence on the general teen-age crowd culture.)

Columnist Inez Robb writes about the experience of her adult friends with a teen-age party: "My husband and I simply weren't prepared for what happened. And to think that all the boys were from good preparatory schools and the girls from the best finishing schools. . . . What really defeated my friend, however, was not the roughhousing or the drinking, no matter how little she condoned it. . . . She was so shocked by the heavy, uninhibited necking that she finally told the committee it must stop at once and that . . . the party was over."

But did she complain to any of the other parents, Miss Robb asked. No. She and her husband were afraid that the other parents and their children might "take it out" on their son. The loss of popularity is a serious threat.

It seems almost unfair to single out any community because hundreds of others have parallel stories to tell. But the case is documented by recent history in Scarsdale, New York. A Parent-Teacher Association meeting was convened to discuss a problem which is assuming critical proportions in a growing number of communities: the teen-age open-house party. As elsewhere, there had been a rash of incidents, including considerable property damage and some personal injuries. In the fall of 1961, the police had to be called for help five times. It is not at all unusual, incidentally, for suburban police to provide officers to regulate traffic for teen-age parties.

The P.T.A. president gave a brief "historical" account of the evolution of the open-house party. "The current form of party which seems most acceptable to adolescents is a modification of the adult open-house with the word 'open' rather loosely interpreted," she said. "The only things 'open' about adult parties are the times of arrival and departure. To youngsters 'open' means everyone is invited."

An "expert" on teen-age mores in another New York suburban community—she has teen-age children herself and currently serves on a committee which is trying to resolve problems similar to those of Scarsdale—explained that the reason for the "open-house" trend is that teen-agers are afraid of losing popularity if they limit their invitations to their friends. A large party is not only a status symbol but a way of buying personal favor, and the number of people who show up is used as a tangible popularity index. In addition, there is an element of fear: the uninvited have been known to "invade" or crash the party, sometimes through windows and unopened French doors, adding to the damage.

Back to Scarsdale! Testimony revealed that 150 to 170 teen-agers have appeared at these parties. Intense rivalry has opened competition for sheer mass attendance.

A report in the local newspaper, *The Scarsdale Inquirer,* said 125 mothers blamed "insecurity, rebellion, inactivity, a lack of community facilities, group pressures and pseudo maturity" as possible causes of the current wave of teen-age party-crashing. It is interesting that the first four of those "possible causes" were used to "explain" the rise in juvenile delinquency in slum sections after World War II.

With the typical overtones of adult helplessness, the P.T.A. president said: "We're concerned with our responsibility as parents. What are some of the positive things we can do? Is this what we or the youngsters want? And have we let our children know how we feel?"

What are the steps a community takes in such cases, if this meeting is to be taken as typical? First, there is the protest that things are not as serious as the reports might make them appear because "most of the incidents are caused by a teen-age minority." Then there is extensive discussion. The elementary school psychologist led a conference panel which "the P.T.A. hopes will result in further talks between parents and adolescents." It is proposed that the teen-agers have their own debate of the issue. Finally, the meeting was informed that the police had suggested that they be notified in advance of large parties so that they can patrol the area. In addition, it was learned, off-duty policemen can be hired to control traffic and, if necessary, prevent vandalism.

These "remedies" speak for themselves. So does much of the diffident tenor of the adult discussion. One woman suggested that the very act of calling the meeting without first getting the views of the teen-agers showed "feelings of confusion and inadequacy on the part of the adults." Adult opinion indeed appeared confused. While one mother whose son had been crashing parties saw nothing wrong with it ("It was just something to do on Friday or Saturday night, and everybody was doing it."), several others described incidents in their homes, which included egg-throwing by "crashers" and $3,000 in damage done by regular "guests."

But the meeting also gave an insight into the specifics of adult abdication of responsibility to adolescents. As in other communities with similar problems, it became clear that parents had frequently left their homes, unchaperoned by themselves or any other adults, to their teen-age children and friends. In addition, many parents had made no effort to know the whereabouts of their children—obviously in the mistaken view that teen-agers no longer are children for whom they are responsible.

One unidentified mother probably got close to the heart of the matter. "So much has been provided here for youngsters' amusement that they no longer know how to entertain themselves without becoming bizarre. Each parent should look at himself, and see which of his attitudes is reflected in his children."

It is important to understand trends rather than symptoms and specific events. Youngsters who as pre-school children are "entertained" at infants' parties by magicians and other professionals, who have grown up with movies and television at their unlimited and uncensored beck and call, who have been admired by their families for being adult rather than naturally childish in their interests—these youngsters can only be expected to be unable to cope with time and leisure—and even friends—on their hands.

"The trend to start children's social life at earlier ages was criticized by some adults," said the Scarsdale report. "They felt that sixth grade was too soon to begin social dancing." Dr. Penelope P. Pollaczek, school psychologist, asked the key question: "Why are we so anxious for our children to become adults at an early age?" She might have added, "Adults in body, but not in mind."

New York Times reporter Martin Tolchin told of one Connecticut mother who rebelled when friends tried to make her be "reasonable" and let her thirteen-year-old daughter date. "They're not little girls, but little old ladies," she said. "I tell my daughter when she's sixteen, she'll be the new girl in town." It is a sound, but currently not very popular theory, and the lady from Connecticut deserves credit for risking not being "well-liked."

It is, furthermore, a theory which apparently is not making much headway, in suburb or city. (The sociologists tend to blame most of the excessive crowd pressures on suburban living, but the cities are by no means immune.) The *New York Times* reported pictorially on the dance dress for the fashionable eighth-grader, worn at a "Roaring Twenties" dance, billed as a benefit. It is interesting, if a little depressing, that the "Roaring Twenties," which were after all roaring for the college crowd and young adults, seemed the suitable theme for youngsters just in the very beginning of their teens—children who would still have been in elementary school before the junior high school began to spread the illusion of maturity. The Twist competed in popularity with the Charleston. Many girls, the report said, had professionally coiffed hairdos. And the boys "were uniformly attired in conservative Brooks Brothers suits."

The daring lady from Connecticut might take note of the fact that, alongside the thirteen-year-old little old ladies there are also suitably uniformed little old men.

4 *Early Marriage: High Cost of Loving*

Dating in elementary school and going steady in junior high inevitably have led to early marriage. The "trend" has been helped along by general affluence (which has removed economic barriers from the biological and social drive toward setting up house); by parental protectiveness (which has made it almost routine for parents, if they can afford it, to finance young marriages); by increased job opportunities for young women (which have made it easy for the girl to be a breadwinner, too).

The statistical facts are plain. In mid-1961, the Population Reference Bureau reported that nearly 40 per cent of all brides in the United States were teen-agers. In 1958, it was reported, 39 per cent of all brides and 12 per cent of all grooms were under twenty, compared with 32 per cent and 7 per cent respectively in 1950. On the extreme side, in 1958 almost two thousand girls married before they reached their fifteenth birthday. The "preferred age" for marriage appears to be eighteen for girls and twenty-one for boys. One out of four college students in the United States today is married. Harvard University reports that, while it has not yet reached that national married student average, it is rapidly moving toward it.

There is nothing wrong—or very new—about early marriage. In many previous civilizations, teen-age marriage was considered the norm, not the exception. Early marriage was a custom of eighteenth-century Europe, and it extended well into the nineteenth century. Ophelia, as created by Shakespeare, was thought to be a girl of about fourteen. In primitive tribes, children in their young teens are still considered ready for the independence of marriage.

In each instance, however, readiness for independence was the key, more important to the idea of marriageability than actual age. The married children in the tribe gave notice that they were ready to fend for themselves. Whatever their mental and intellectual flaws, the speech, thoughts and general level of literacy of either Hamlet or Ophelia can hardly be called teen-age. And the hillbilly child bride was considered a full-fledged, "mature" member of the low life and general misery of that particular backwater of civilization.

But modern middle-class America, until very recently, considered early marriage as something of a lower-class phenomenon. It happened, of course, in middle- and upper-middle-class families, but it was not encouraged. This was reflected, for example, in the strict prohibition against married students in most of the good women's colleges. Marriage in high school was even more completely out of the question.

All this has changed radically. The trend toward married college students has been gathering momentum for some time. It was given its strongest support after World War II, when veterans virtually took over the campuses, thus replacing the traditional college boy in his late teens with mature men who had seen not only battle but life. Pregnant women, baby carriages, and "family units" in quonset huts became as much part of "college life" as ivy-covered halls and fraternity rows had been during the previous generation.

In the years that followed, the ways of the veterans remained, in large measure, the ways of college students, even though entering freshmen were once again sixteen- to eighteen-year-olds. Moreover, the greatly increased flow from college to professional or graduate school began to blur the distinction between collegiate and university life. What was good for the medical intern in his late twenties came to be considered equally acceptable for the undergraduates. From the practical point of view, it was often easier since the college student still had the full benefit of parental support and his life was a good deal less hectic and insecure than that of the young medical or law student.

As in all other matters, the marriage habit was steadily pushed downward, to lower levels of age and maturity. When the debate over whether it was proper to be married and a mother before college graduation was resolved in the affirmative, it moved down into the high schools where it now rages. The age group currently under discussion is that of the fifteen- to seventeen-year-olds.

What has sparked the trend?

The most obvious and overt reason is in the general approval of hothouse social development of young Americans. Early dating and constant preoccupation with romance and sex could lead nowhere else. What is left for teen-agers after the experience of "going steady?" To expect anything but early marriage is like encouraging young engagements and believing they will just dissolve.

We are not likely ever to have accurate statistics about the number of teen-age marriages which were the direct consequence of sexual intercourse and pregnancy among "steadies." But much more important than whether teen-age mothers are the necessity of the invention of teen-age marriage is the fact that even without the necessity, pressure to take the next step is strong.

These children have been brought up on the philosophy of instant gratification. Some psychologists say this is desirable. They point to the insecurity of today's world, to the fears that tomorrow there will be atomic holocaust. A greater historical perspective might balance these fears with the knowledge of a vastly increased statistical likelihood of a long and medically protected life. Atomic disaster is far less of a probability for most of today's youngsters than death by plague or famine was for their counterparts a few hundred years ago.

Whatever the rationalizations, these youngsters have been brought up on the theory that it is better to postpone intellectual maturity than sociability and fun. The individual's pursuit of happiness, in addition to being a safeguarded liberty under the Constitution, has been sanctioned as a priority, if not full-time, occupation. In the sex-soaked atmosphere that surrounds teen-agers, how could anything less than early marriage cash in on the guarantee of happiness?

In the absence of any training in the art of timing, youngsters want what is available and desirable—and they want it now. In a crowd-dominated atmosphere, trends advance with unnatural speed. Earl H. Hanson, superintendent of schools in Rock Island, Illinois, quotes a recently engaged high school student: "My sister got married when her boy friend went into the service, and look at her now. Three swell kids, a nice air-conditioned house, a dishwasher and a washer-dryer. Why shouldn't I do the same thing? Joe loves me now, but if he gets off to college first, those co-eds might make him forget me."

Much of the drive toward early marriage is probably an unconscious desire to "show" one's parents that adolescence and dependence are a thing of the past. "You have to treat me as grown-up if I'm married," is almost an implied threat. But if the declaration of independence is followed by continued fiscal dependence, the sham triumph leads to a terrible psychological letdown. This can harm permanently not only the youngsters' relationships with the parents but deliver a fatal blow to the young marrieds' self-esteem and confidence —and thereby destroy their marriage. This is comparable to the contrast between the wild independence festivities of some of the new African underdeveloped nations, followed by humiliating inability to make independence work without help from the more fully developed nations. The analogy could be carried a step further: it is unquestionably the fault of the "adult" nations that they have so long neglected the education and training of the "young" countries, leaving them so unprepared for the independence they so understandably sought.

Whatever the pressures of the crowd may have done to make young marriage popular, the additional matriarchal pressures cannot be overlooked. The mothers of girls influence the girls' impatience to be safely married and thus rush the clock. An Eastern school superintendent said: "It's indecent the way the mothers beam when their elementary school children trundle off hand-in-hand on their dates." Another educator said that mothers not only condone but urge their daughters' catching of steady boy friends. Dr. Hanson tells the story of a high school dean cautioning a young girl against getting married too hastily. The same evening the girl's mother, outraged, telephoned the dean. "What are you trying to do? Get my girl and her boy friend disengaged?"

A professor at one of the country's outstanding colleges tells of an interview with one of his most brilliant and promising seniors. He congratulated the student on winning a coveted study award for a year's research abroad.

"I don't think I'm going to take it," said the student. The professor thought he had misunderstood, but the student insisted that he could not take the grant. "She doesn't want me to go," he said.

The professor said he was surprised to learn that the

student was married. The boy shook his head—somewhat wistfully, the teacher thought—and said that "she" was his steady girl.

"I made him sign the papers of that grant right then and there in my office," said the teacher. He wanted to make sure that the impatient, selfish demands of an immature girl would not stand in the way of another promising young man. Moreover, he was sufficiently convinced that the boy was waiting for a hint of adult encouragement to stand up against the pressures for early marriage.

Many youngsters never get such encouragement.

Society always justifies its actions. American society, through the absolute mastery of public relations and mass communications, has made a science of the justification of popular practice. While the glorification of the inevitable may help to prevent unnecessary recriminations and guilt complexes, it also makes it that much more difficult for others to swim against the stream, much less reverse a national trend.

As already indicated, the trend toward college marriage was started by the veterans returning to the campus. These older students, with the habits of adults, were at first regarded with suspicion and some downright hostility. But when they turned out to be superior students, largely because of their greater maturity and sense of purpose, they came to be the example both for the younger crowd and for the educators, who were understandably relieved to have found an audience that did not need to be convinced about the importance of education.

These young men were mature about their study and they also were adult about their social and sex life. Theirs was an adult community, largely grouped around the nucleus of married couples. They were no longer preoccupied with the crucial question of the Saturday-night date. They were less likely to rush off campus the minute the last Friday lecture was adjourned. They had seen the world of war, travel, excitement, and now they were trying to get every ounce of intellectual value out of college to prepare for jobs, vocations and professions.

It should have been considered natural that these new students acted like adults: they were adult. It was less reasonable and perceptive to conclude that because these older students did well in spite of early marriage it would follow that their successors who, after all, were once again teen-agers would do as well under similar circumstances. In fact, what was a boon to the veterans, may very well be a great hindrance to the regular college student. Yet, colleges are so anxious not to offend public opinion or to go counter to the widely accepted trend that they stand ready to pour vast amounts of money into the planning of married students' quarters, not for graduate students only but for undergraduates as well. Aside from the huge financial burden thus added to the already staggering need for the expansion of higher education, the real issue of this trend is in its infectiousness. Superficially viewed, the lure of a "model apartment" and its favorable comparision with the dormitory room speaks eloquently for finding a mate, setting up house and getting all the extra benefits of a home on the campus. In adult life, the advantages of family living are, of course, beyond question. The question is whether the settled life of home and hearth is the best arrangement for undergraduate education. If the answer is Yes, what possible excuse then remains for the institution of the college campus itself? Would it not be far more economical and educationally no less effective to have classrooms and lecture halls in the vicinity of a series of Levittowns and similar housing developments?

If the trend toward college marriage is a mixed blessing, its filtering down to the high school and junior high school level is more serious. As indicated, the apologists try to make a case for high school marriages, saying that they ensure less promiscuity and greater chastity; but in too many instances this argument is comparable to that of the man who jumps out of the window because he is afraid of life. In a typical attempt to justify the constructive aspects of early marriage, *The Family Life Coordinator,* a quarterly journal published at the University of Oregon, charges that emotional and disapproving public response to high school marriages cast an unnecessary curse on these unions. It is because such marriages are often targets of community hostility, the argument goes, that so many of them fail. They are expected to fail.

Whatever the reasons, teen-age marriages do fail alarmingly often. Divorce and annulment rates are higher than for the population as a whole. Bureau of Census figures show that divorces are 12.6 per cent for women married between the ages of fifteen and nineteen, compared with 4.8 per cent for those married between twenty-one and twenty-five. One study, conducted by the National Education Association, showed that of 240 high-school-age marriages followed up for this particular survey, only sixteen survived.

Even those who are trying hard—probably too hard for the good of teen-age society—to find reasons why high school marriages are a good thing, have trouble with such statistics. A discussion of the issue in *The Bulletin on Family Development* asks: "Is the high divorce rate for early marriages due to factors inherent in early marriage itself or due to the fact that society, having decided early marriage is bad, proceeds to destroy it? Is it not probable that the young-marrieds, saturated wtih foreboding, start to see problems around every corner where none exist? In fact, some young couples who are reasonably well adjusted might begin to think that there is indeed something unnatural about their relationship inasmuch as they do not live up to the model expectation of being beset with problems?"

One might counter this question with the inquiry why, if society is really so successful in destroying early marriages because it so strongly disapproves of them, it has been so unsuccessful in preventing them in the first place? In fact, that part of society which has its strongest impact on young people, both before and after marriage, not only does not disapprove of early marriage but, as has been shown before, plants its seeds and hothouse-nurtures them to fruition on the teen-age wedding day.

The Princeton senior who, speaking anonymously in *The Unsilent Generation,* describes his frantic efforts to remain a bachelor through his teen years, may be a good deal closer to the true estimate of society's pressures. "Women are such predatory creatures," he complains. "They are always anxious to get married as fast as possible and to raise a flock of kids. And they're often not very subtle in showing their desires. As a result, my typical dating experience has been something like this: I take a girl out and we find that we have much in common and are very compatible; we go out on two or three further dates and find we are becoming very fond of each other; she sweetly takes me window-shopping for engagement rings, bedroom sets, and bassinets."

The problem continues to become more and more serious. Recent studies showed that high school marriages have become an important factor in the drop-out trend—youngsters leaving school before graduation, with all the later consequences of ruined careers. A statewide study in Iowa showed that 80 per cent of the girls who married in high school dropped out and only 8 per cent of them eventually came back. Of the boys, 43 per cent who married left school, and only 9 per cent of them returned to the classroom. Although at the time of the survey, the Iowa girls on an average had only been married for six months, more than half of them said they were sorry they had married before finishing school. Underlining the problem of immature teen-age sex-experimentation, the study also found 39 per cent of the girls who had married in high school were pregnant before their wedding and that the overwhelming majority of them regretted their marriages. The confusion of these youngsters and the lack of proper and firm guidance by the adult community was driven home by the variety of reasons they gave for wanting to get married: unhappy homes and dissatisfaction with school, sexual infatuation, the need to prove themselves "grown-up" and unrealistic romantic notions that "love solves all problems." (One college senior adds another clue to that aspect of the confusion. "Sure, I'll marry for love," he wrote. "Whatever that may be.")

An indication of the serious realities of increasing numbers of high school marriages is the growing concern by school administrators with the legal aspects of the problem. Some educators feel that, by excluding married students from school, they may deter others from marrying. They add that if the permissiveness continues, the mere fact that married students are part of the crowd will make the remainder of the crowd more likely to follow their "example."

But since—commendably—compulsory education up to age sixteen is so strong a tradition, the number of school people who take a strong stand against married students is getting less every year. In Dallas, where married students used to be excluded from school, the P.T.A. counsel recommended the establishment of separate schools for married students. Dallas points to the accomplished fact: in 1953, there were 59 married students in the city's schools; in 1957, the number had risen to 286, and by 1959 there were 480—twelve of them in junior high school and nine in elementary schools.

Some cities solve the problem by recommending that married students attend evening school. Others, among them Washington, send husband and wife to different schools in order to deemphasize the fact that these are married couples. Another group of cities allows married students to stay in school but excludes them from extracurricular activities. A number of cities, including Detroit, Providence and Wichita, make no distinction between married and unmarried students. Oakland, California, does not bar pregnant girls, married or unmarried, although pregnant students may receive instruction at home.

Ironically, while most school spokesmen have given in to what they consider irresistible pressures, some of the most selective colleges have made a stronger stand. Swarthmore, for instance, still enforces the rule that, if two of its students get married, one of them must withdraw from the college.

It would be foolish and irresponsible to label all early marriages as ill-considered and undesirable. Young people mature according to a very erratic and individualistic timetable. It is quite possible for a teen-ager to be more mature than some young adults in their twenties. Any study of successful and prominent persons will include a number who married their childhood sweethearts in their teens and whose early choice turned out to be the right one.

But this is not the question at issue. The heart of the matter is that social pressures and the ways of the tyrannical teen-age crowd are putting a premium on premature marriages. In an article for the *Carnegie Alumnus*, Margaret Mead, the anthropologist and outspoken social critic, warns that young people who marry before their formal education is completed "have no chance to find themselves in college because they have clung to each other exclusively. They can take little advantage of college as a broadening experience and they often show less breadth of vision as seniors than they did as freshmen. They marry, whether as undergraduates or immediately upon graduation, have children in quick succession, and retire to the suburbs to have more children. . . . At thirty, they are still immature and dependent, their future mortgaged for twenty or thirty years ahead, neither husband nor wife realizing the promise that a different kind of undergraduate life might have enabled them to fulfill."

Miss Mead finds it hard to tell which sex loses more, the boys who just had a glimpse of what "freedom to achieve" might mean, or the girls who are kept fixed on the absolute necessity of a man—so that they never get even a glimpse of the real challenge. These are the girls who go to school, not to pursue learning, but to learn pursuing. They are not alone to blame; they know full well that many parents are investing in their daughters' education so that they can catch a college-educated man.

These are the real dangers. The more tangible ones are more easily described and understood. The fact, for instance, that girls marrying before the age of eighteen have almost twice as many children than women marrying in their twenties, is a reality. These girls not only are divorced more readily but also are more likely to be unhappy about their marriages. It follows that this trend will give to our society, which already subjects a cruel number of its children to the torture of growing up in in broken or unhappy homes, a surplus harvest of maladjusted, lost and neurotic children.

In the long run, however, the intangible losses may be even more damaging because they are harder to counteract. The marriage that failed is open to public inspection. The opportunity never taken is not only lost but its loss is never fully known. The natural pressures in a technological age of vast financial, industrial and governmental enterprises are in the direction of security rather than adventure. A society which hires not single employees but corporation couples, and which wants to rate the wives of naval officers along with their husbands—that society, for better or for worse, offers limited scope for daring experimentation once a young man or woman has become part of the adult production and consumption machine.

This is why it ought to be considered doubly important that the young, during the maturing process, take full advantage of intellectual probing, experimentation and searching. It is in school and college that the opportunity to learn to know oneself and others is not, as it inevitably will be later on, related to economic gain or loss. This could be the time of a measure of intellectual independence that, for most adults, will never come again. Yet, the Bureau of Social Science Research found that early marriage is becoming a serious obstacle to the completion of graduate study; industrial recruiters in colleges say that an increasing number of students look for the secure job with the most promising retirement benefits, rather than the kind of work in which they might combine the excitement of risk with the outside chance of really satisfying success; and high schools—even junior high schools—find it hard, if not impossible, to stem the tide of those who want to play at being grown-up, without first growing up.

This last group is most to be pitied. In what is often an only vaguely understood rebellion against dependence on their parents teen-agers maneuver themselves into a position of far greater dependence—either on continued parental subsidy or on breadwinning without long-range aim or promise. For those who are not really in love, the premature marriage can hold out nothing but misery. For those who truly love each other and are suited for marriage, postponement always was a hardship, though not necessarily an undesirable one in the long run. Unfortunately, postponement of desired pleasures now seems almost un-American. The saddest thought of all is that, as early hothouse-grown marriages become the accepted way of life, teen-agers in future generations may not even know the genuine happiness they might pursue, if only they gave themselves time to grow up.

5 *Teen-Age Maturity Symbols: Smoking, Drinking, Cars*

There is no doubt about the amount of teen-age smoking: a great deal too much. The issue is no longer the age-old one of parents vaguely feeling that it just "isn't good for kids" to smoke. It is now scientifically proven that smoking and lung cancer (and probably a number of other diseases, including those of the heart) are intimately linked. Nor is there any question that the most serious aspect of the cigarette's impact on health is the length of time over which a person uses tobacco in quantity. The cigarette smoker who has consumed great quantities of cigarettes regularly since early adulthood is more likely to face serious trouble later on. It follows that the boy or girl who started the habit in the early teens is an even poorer health risk forty or fifty years later.

Changing Times, the Kiplinger magazine, reported that the number of children reaching "smoking age" is larger and the age when smoking becomes a regular habit is getting steadily lower. It is interesting that a generation which knows far more about science than its elders and which, according to the school psychologists, ascribes most of its shortcomings and maladjustments to fear of an untimely death through atomic fall-out or nuclear war seems to have so little concern about protecting itself against a far greater probability of doom through cancer.

The American Cancer Society questioned 22,000 students in the Portland, Oregon, area and found that one out of every four high school boys and one out of every eight girls smoked. The number of smokers increased with every year of high school, so that among seniors 35.4 per cent of the boys and 26.2 per cent of the girls were found to be smoking.

In Newton, Massachusetts, 6,810 high school students were polled: a quarter of the boys and fifth of the girls smoked in a survey of all grades from seventh through senior year. By senior year approximately half of all students—boys and girls—were smokers, with some of them reporting that they had become "regular smokers" at ages eight and nine.

Another study in Levittown, Long Island, confirmed the general trend of these statistics. Of those who were smokers, 59 per cent said they began before they were fifteen years old. The largest number had started smoking at age fourteen.

Why do teen-agers smoke? The reasons given by the youngsters themselves usually are "social," meaning the desire to appear sophisticated and adult. Inevitably, the children of parents who are smokers are more likely to become smokers themselves, regardless how much the parents may disapprove. Most parents, at any rate, appear to bow to the inevitable: 70 per cent of the smoking teen-agers said they had obtained parental permission about a year after they had begun to smoke regularly.

Schools are very concerned about what is professionally referred to as "the smoking problem." A great deal of time is spent, much of it fruitlessly, in discussion of the issue. Education journals frequently deal with it at length.

As with all other undesirable actions of teen-agers, including early marriage, opinion is divided between those who say that since smoking is a fact of teen-age life, allowance should be made for it, and those who would like to stop the habit, even though this might make them unpopular. The permissive group frequently asks that a special time and place be set aside in high schools—a smoking break and a students' smoking lounge—where cigarettes may be lit legally. The theory is that prohibition merely leads to law-breaking, smoking in toilets and fire hazards. The counter argument is that by sanctioning smoking the pressures on the nonsmokers to conform to the mores of the crowd become even stronger and the chances of parents to stand up and set their own standards get slimmer. This debate is not confined to the public schools. The alumni magazine of one of the country's most prominent boys' academies argued the issue with vehement seriousness.

If it were not for those questions and the over-all picture of letting the predominant crowd pressure dictate what is right and wrong, the amount of time and effort spent on the smoking business would merely be ludicrous.

A high school principal in Norwalk, Connecticut, who wanted to impose tighter smoking restrictions ran into a storm of protest. Student opinion was varied and articulate. One teen-ager said: "Whether a student smokes should be his own business. I can understand their [the school's] prohibiting smoking as a fire regulation within the building. But what right have they to control a student's habits when he is on private property. . . . The school isn't satisfied with its role as educator. It wants to assume the job of parent as well." (There is a strong ingredient of psychological analysis in this remark—the semiunderstood playback that is increasingly prominent in teen-age rationalizations.)

A teen-age girl reacted: "If the teachers have a faculty room in which to smoke, then we ought to be given a place where we can relax and have a smoke without disturbing anyone. We'd be just as careful as the teachers are." (Quite aside from the question of smoking, here is the logical consequence of a generation brought up as "pals" by teachers as well as parents. The theory of "equal rights," without special privileges based on age, experience or seniority, is deeply ingrained in this approach to life and education.)

In the absence of the school's authority, or its desire to establish it, the adult methods of committee rule are given a whirl. In Mamaroneck, Westchester County, New York, for example, a program has been worked out, with a good deal of publicity. A group of boys and girls formed a Committee on Smoking, as an experiment in educating teen-agers as to the hazards of the weed. Literature is distributed. Posters are put up. Slides and films are shown. Smoking is not prohibited in the town's schools, but the students take an annual vote and then request the Board of Education to give permission for the year only. As for the educational campaign and perhaps by way of summary of the entire problem—some high school seniors said: "If the program is to succeed, start with the junior high schools. It's too late for us—we're hooked."

There is a fundamental difference between the problem of teen-age smoking and the related one of drinking: whatever may be wrong about smoking, it harms only the individual; drinking may pose serious dangers, not only to the one who drinks but to those around him, including many innocent bystanders.

As with dating, sex experimentation, early marriage and smoking, the liquor problem has dripped down from college to high school and below. It is generally, though by no means gladly, acknowledged that adolescents today drink and that this must be taken into consideration in any frank discussion of teen-age behavior. Nearly all the advice books include chapters on the subject. The national estimate of the proportion of teen-agers who drink more or less regularly is between 50 and 66 per cent. As with all other unpleasant facts about teen-age behavior, many parents pretend that they are unaware of the problem. Most parents tend to assure any inquiring researcher that they would not serve liquor to their children and friends, at least not without supervision, and that they would not permit their children to drink away from home.

This is not the way things work out in practice. Thelma Purtell, in her book, "*The Intelligent Parent's Guide to Teen-Agers,* says that one of the agreements on teen-age behavior, the Parents League Code, had to be rewritten recently to give more stress to the dangers of alcohol and to formulate stronger rules to help families cope with the problem. She adds: "In a society that accepts adult drinking, it is natural that teen-agers, in making demands for adult prerogatives, should include the right to find out for themselves about liquor as well as everything else. Drinking by teen-agers, beyond the family circle, constitutes another form of experimentation in the business of becoming an adult."

In some Westchester communities, groups of sophisticated parents tried to solve the liquor problem by serving the drinks themselves after a graduation fling. When the town got wind of the "experiment," it was abandoned. But it is, of course, no secret that many parents continue the practice on their own.

Nor is the issue exclusively one for New York suburbs. A *New York Times* story described a controversy over teen drinking in Rose Valley, "a normally placid community tucked away in the woods of suburban Delaware County, a few miles from Philadelphia." Rose Valley was in turmoil over a proposal to permit supervised drinking at occasional dances for teen-agers who have graduated from high school. The proposal was submitted by the Rose Valley Folk, "a civic and social organization formed by artists and other professional people who wanted to get away from Philadelphia's urban ways." Possibly they were better at taking those ways with them than in leaving them behind.

According to the Rose Valley plan, the youngsters were to bring their own bottles, but anyone wanting a drink was to ask his parents or a chaperone for permission. The adults were to do the bartending.

Those who approve of this kind of "solution"—such as the Colorado family that served champagne to twenty youngsters after high school graduation or a group of parents who advocate spiking the punch for teen parties—argue that it is better for youngsters to drink under the watchful eye of adults than to sneak out and drink in secret, without controls.

The father of a fifteen-year-old high school girl and head of a well-to-do, conservative New England household told with dismay that his daughter, when asked why she was back so early from a Friday night double date, said: "Janie got sick after she drank too much and we had to transport her home." Janie was a fifteen-year-old classmate of similar parental background. The father, unable to hide his concern, asked whether it was customary for the teen-age group to drink. His daughter, apparently anxious to reassure him, said that she herself never drank too much and had only had two Scotches that night. Needless to say, Dad was not reassured. But, he asked, what could he do?

How do teen-agers themselves feel about the matter? A Gallup survey found them to be "tolerant." Most of them approve of moderate or social drinking, and a large number of them said they did drink. Almost half of the college students said their companions "drink a lot." More than 20 per cent of the high school seniors and 10 per cent of the sophomores and working youths of similar age reported about the same habits as the college students.

Drinking on graduation night is increasingly considered the ceremonial entry into the adult world. But the real story of dangerous teen-age drinking usually follows the official graduation party. A Georgia teen-ager described such a brawl in the *Atlanta Constitution*: "We began our party at a night spot where mixed drinks are served, and progressed from one club to another. After we all had a few drinks, we went to a lake cottage owned by one of the boys' parents. We took along our own liquor and sat around and talked, played records and drank. There were no chaperones. After a while, couples wandered off to the water's edge, into the woods, or a side room. We felt that after graduation from high school we were adults and could do anything adults could do, and were out to prove it."

Time and again, it is suggested that youngsters drink only

to keep up with the crowd. Ann Landers advises that, when this appears to be happening to a teen-ager, he should change his crowd. Some psychologists contradict the entire theory, insist instead that a teen-ager joins the kind of crowd he likes, the kind that "fills his needs." This implies that he ought to join a drinking crowd because he likes to drink and wants company.

None of this gets even close to the root of the problem. It is sadly ironic that American public opinion tends to swing from one ridiculous extreme to the other. It sounds unbelievable that the country which foolishly and arrogantly thought it could prohibit the sale and use of alcoholic beverages to the entire population, regardless of age and maturity, now appears to feel that there is no way to lay down the law about drinking to children and adolescents. Part of that reluctance is the subconscious feeling that adult society, in order to "have a right" to legislate to teen-agers, would have to give up its own cocktails.

This is nonsense. It is the kind of nonsense that confuses the issues between the roles of teen-agers and adults all across the board. While excessive drinking among adults cannot be condoned (quite apart from any question of its impact on teen-agers), to insist that nothing that is approved for adults can be prohibited for teen-agers would play havoc with both adolescent and adult life.

There are two separate approaches to the alcohol problem, both important in counteracting the trend. The first is purely educational. It tells young people what the facts about alcohol are. Ralph W. Daniel, executive director of the Michigan State Board of Alcoholism, points out that children do, of course, get a good deal of "alcohol education" of a kind—"liquor advertisements, motion pictures, and television are educating them about alcohol."

Mr. Daniel continues: "A child should be told why some people drink and why others abstain. He should be told why there are laws prohibiting teen-age drinking. Someday he will make his own decision, and we should give him the tools that will enable him to make a decision that will be right for him. It should be a decision that he can be sure about, one that he can live with comfortably. Our children do not have to inherit our hangover of indecision."

Important though this part of the solution is, it is only an incomplete approach. Schools may lecture about alcohol. They may show slides pointing out what alcohol does to the insides of a drunkard's stomach. The main task remains to be done at home.

That job merely runs parallel to all the other adult responsibilities in an effort to return from chaotic permissiveness to enlightened authority. The father who says: "I am not to be stampeded into serving drinks to a bunch of under-age kids and I am not going to give up my cocktail," is much closer to the solution than those who try to make us believe that adolescents can be made to give up drinking only if adults abstain too. (The latter approach, applied also to the problem of sex relations, might solve the danger of the population explosion and, in the process, wipe out the human race altogether. We are not afraid that this will happen, but it is a good illustration of the idiocy of the attempt to make adults conform to teen-age ways in order not to "corrupt" teen-agers.)

Some parents complain that while they themselves would like to lay down the law about drinking, few of the other parents are interested, or even in sympathy. One father tells of an evening when a group of boys "in a gay mood" crashed a neighborhood party. The host became alarmed and tried to reach the parents of some of the youngsters by phone. None were home. Finally, in desperation, he called a neighbor whom he knew to be friendly with the parents of one of the party-crashers. On the following morning, the other parents expressed nothing but anger and disapproval over the host's action. When told that they were fortunate that a call to the police had been avoided, they were highly indignant.

The moral of this story is that it does, indeed, take courage to move against the stream. It is not coincidental that shortly after his space flight, when astronaut John H. Glenn and a local minister in a suburb near Washington were booed and assaulted for trying to stop a group of teen-age party-crashers, the only reaction was one of "reassurance" that the boys had not actually recognized the Colonel. Presumably, they did know the local minister, however, and refused to permit his presence to dampen their beer-bolstered spirits. The fact that they had been drinking was offered as—an excuse.

The only answer, unpleasant as it may sound, is in parental courage—whether or not the majority of the other parents initially approve. One mother documents this with her story:

"At a beach party last summer, some boys who hadn't been invited crashed the party and arrived with beer. I didn't even realize it at first—I had never had the problem as the children were only fifteen and sixteen—but the party seemed to be getting out of hand. My husband and I checked and found the beer cache. We confiscated every bit, and sent the crashers home, although up until then I had felt sorry for them and had been inclined to let them stay. I even had to call the mother of one girl to come and get her. I explained exactly what happened, although I mentioned no names. . . . No, it didn't ruin my child's social life. The whole gang was back on the porch the next night, and the next and the next."

As with many other teen-age customs, there is good reason to believe that the youngsters are, in fact, waiting for some limits to be set by adult authority. In one survey, for example, over half of the youngsters who said they did drink also added that they would not drink at all if none of their friends did. It would be naïve to suggest that if limits are set, none of the teen-agers will transgress and risk punishment. But to make this an argument against asserting adult authority is equivalent to saying that there should be no laws as long as there is danger that they will be broken. It is in the absence of clearly defined rules that teen-agers are actually driven to prove how far they may go, and often they will become conscious of their mistakes only after they have reached a point of no return.

Unless adults summon the courage of their responsibilities, it is only a matter of time before school committees will debate whether school buildings should have cocktail lounges for students where they may drink without causing disturbances and without secrecy. The issue of the smoking lounge by then will have been settled "in favor" of the teen-agers. The argument on behalf of the cocktail lounge will undoubtedly be that since their fathers and mothers are free to have a drink before lunch, it would be unfair, undemocratic and repressive not to grant equal rights to adolescents.

The automobile is more than a means of transportation. To the nation it is one of the most important indexes of prosperity, and even a switch from large cars to compact models can sufficiently affect the production of steel and oil to help lead into a recession. To many citizens the car is a status symbol. For some of the minority groups, who are tragically denied equal opportunities in housing, the car is the only outward sign of equality. To youth, it is recreation hall, freedom and mobility, front porch and boudoir. "Parking," in teen-age language, means petting or more. Lovers' Lanes tend to be rows of parked cars rather than idyllic garden paths. When the students in a well-known coeducational college fought for the right to maintain cars on campus, one of the leaders admitted privately: "We don't even mind whether the cars have wheels. Just as long as they have doors."

One long-term observer of college life said that although everybody discusses the many changes of the curriculum and their influence on higher education, nobody seems to realize that the single most important impact on the college community has been made by the car. While it used to be argued that campus life, outside the classrooms and especially during weekends, was the most important ingredient of a college education, too little of this leisurely way of academic living has survived: weekends are marked by an almost total exodus, and the evacuation has been made possible by the car. A few colleges, such as Princeton and Oberlin, have had the courage to continue the ban against automobiles. Most of the women's colleges restrict the privilege of on-campus cars to the senior class, although the preponderance of dates who own cars has motorized the majority of the girls anyway.

Today's teen-agers are the first generation to have grown up with cars as an indispensable part of the family. The only thing more desirable than a "family car" is a "two-car garage." Everything is geared to life on wheels. Teen-agers naturally take the car for granted. They deposit money in drive-in banks. They shop in centers built around parking lots. They visit drive-in movies and eateries. They are driven to parties and dancing lessons in the station wagon. For many teen-agers, brought up in the no-privacy modernity of the family room, the car is the only enclosed area of escape from togetherness.

The commercial image of the car has added glamour to undeniable utility. Girls in bathing suits and svelte models in evening gowns are the natural adornments of almost every automobile ad. The implication is unmistakably that the car is a powerful means of romantic conquest—and few teen-agers would deny the truth of that message.

Power is another lure. Speed, drive and freedom are part of the sales slogans. Every youngster through the ages has dreamed of flying wildly through the world—on fast steeds, on madly dashing stage coaches, on sailing schooners, locomotives and airplanes. But the dreams were always too remote to be translated into reality, except through safe and slow imitations—the river raft, the lumbering wagon and perhaps a canoe in summer.

Now, for the first time, adult power of motion is within the teen-agers' grasp, part of their way of life. The modern automobile, like the performance of the Twist, requires little skill. It offers a great sense of power with a minimum of effort or knowledge. It is designed to give the magic of motion and action without the expenditure of energy. "Going for a drive" is a perfect description.

How many teen-agers actually do have cars? The figures vary. The Gallup survey said 44 per cent of the boys reported having their own cars: 12 per cent of them high school sophomores; 31 per cent high school seniors. Well over half of the college men and 78 per cent of the working youths were car-owners. But in wealthy suburban communities the high school car-ownership is much higher than the average and is thought to be around 75 per cent. The Allstate Insurance Company reports that nationally 75 per cent of all high school juniors and seniors have driver's licenses and nearly 60 per cent have access to the family car for "social purposes."

There are subtle subdivisions in teen-agers' attitudes toward cars. Coleman says the teen-age "elite" uses cars for dating but not to show them off. Other teen-age groups use cars as status symbols in much the same way as teen-age girls moon over Rock 'n' Roll singers. Finally, the world of the hot-rodders is an island unto itself, with mores and values incomprehensible to the uninitiated. *New York Times* reporter Gay Talese says it is impossible to determine accurately the number of hot-rodders in the country. But there are sixteen hot rod magazines on the stands today, with a total monthly circulation of three million.

As in all other areas of tight expertise, the hot-rod elite looks down on the rank and file, whom they call "squirrels." It is the squirrels, they say, who give the hot-rods their deplorable public image. These are "the crazy kids with loud, dual exhausts and a foxtail on their cars. . . . The 'squirrel' doesn't race his car; he's just an exhibitionist. He spins his tires when leaving a drive-in. The real hot-rodder spends all kinds of money preventing his tires from spinning, because spinning tires reduce speed."

According to Talese, most real hot-rodders are just out of their teens and in their early twenties, usually unmarried because "it's an all-consuming hobby." If they get married, they slowly get estranged either from the hot-rod or the wife. They cannot support both, and the really devoted hot-rodder is likely to decide that the wife must go.

But no matter what the differences in youth's attitudes towards the car, all adolescent boys have in common one interest: speed. Drag racing or "dragging" is a popular evening sport, no matter what the rules or the types of cars. A group of motorized boys meet in an appointed spot. At the starting signal (which sometimes is a teen-age girl leaping into the glare of the headlights) they zoom down the "drag strip" often at one hundred miles per hour or more. Involved is the understandable sense of competition plus the assertion of the male ego. One teen-ager said: "We don't drag much when the girls aren't around to watch."

Not all of the boys are exhibitionists, by any means. Motion, speed and excitement are the most natural drives of adolescents, with all their pent-up energy and their need to prove themselves. One boy, when asked why he was interested in drag racing, said: "Why do people have to collect stamps? Look, it's a hobby with us. We like cars. We build engines. We like to see how they hop up, see? And when we drive, there's a thrill. There really is. There's a thrill you can't describe."

The drag racers are, of course, only the minority. The rest, who merely drive, retain one thing in common with the drag set—love of speed. According to the Gallup statistics, more than one fourth of the high school seniors say they have driven faster than ninety miles per hour.

It is not surprising that obsession with speed leads to disaster. The National Safety Council reports that in 1959 teen-agers were involved in twice as many accidents as their numbers would justify. Gallup says that almost 60 per cent of the nation's male youths have been involved in auto accidents, either as passengers or drivers. More than half of the college boys and working youths of the same age have had accidents at the wheel. Perhaps these statistics inspired one major automobile manufacturer to advertise his products as "road-tested by teen-agers." At any rate, the proof of the teen-age car "problem" is in the fact that the young man under twenty (or his parents) sometimes must pay up to three times as much to buy automobile insurance as do "ordinary" drivers.

In addition to the physical hazards, rendered murderous where there is a combination of teen-age drinking and driving, there appears to be serious threat of injury to schoolwork. The Allstate survey found that there is a direct relationship between students' use of cars and failure in their classroom work. Youngsters who use the car four days a week are more than twice as likely to be D students or below than those who only drive two days a week.

Car-ownership, particularly by sixteen-year-olds, is even more catastrophic in academic terms because it often entails holding a job to support the car. There are twice as many A and B students among those who neither own a car nor hold a part-time job than among those who have both car and job. Neither car nor job is harmful by itself, but both in combination spell failure in an alarming number of cases. The pressure of the crowd, led by those who (with the parents' help) can afford to have a car without supporting it, is most damaging to those who want to keep up with their peers but whose parents are unable to foot the bill.

Even more serious, though not visible in the statistics is the support of the car as an incentive to drop out of school. Time and again, educators complain that the car at first leads to a part-time job. Automatically, the greater opportunity for dating and other expenses make the part-time job inadequate to support machine and girl friend in the style to which they would like to become accustomed. The result is a full-time job, drop-out and lifelong reduction of opportunities for advancement.

As in all other aspects of teen-age living, the pattern of parental and educational impotence is apparent. A few years ago, the opening of a new public school in a Connecticut community led to so unmanageable a traffic jam that many commuters missed their trains. When the local police chief asked that the school authorities limit students' use of cars, a Board of Education spokesman said he could do nothing about it since anybody over sixteen years of age is legally entitled to drive. Consequently, the adult community "compromised" by taking earlier trains to clear the roads for teen-age traffic.

News from Connecticut brought testimony from other regions of the country, including the complaint that vast parking lots as part of school planning were driving up costs for school construction and limiting the land available for more beneficial purposes, such as sports grounds. But when one community urged that this noneducational expense be covered by charging parking fees, the superintendent said plaintively that this might lead students to park illegally in residential neighborhoods, thus hurting the school's image in the community. The possibility of laying down rules and then enforcing them apparently occurred to nobody.

How complicated the car issue can become was shown in a report in *School Management*, an educational journal. A superintendent of schools wrote that his school was bothered, not by a parking but an absentee problem. "It seems that many of our students went for a drive during their lunch breaks, returning to their afternoon classes late—and sometimes not at all." After making a survey, the indispensable routine of all educational administration, the authorities decided to restrict the use of students' cars during the school day. The plan sounded sensible, but the machinery of implementing it makes the operation of that school sound more like that of a garage. Office clerks were used to keep track of student-owned cars. A coach and a driving education instructor had to police the parking lot during lunch hour to make sure that students who had parked their cars in the morning did not use them (either for transportation or social purposes) during the school day.

There are no easy answers to the question of teen-age driving in a motorized age. The need for teen-agers to drive varies enormously with the availability of public transportation. But the basic assumption, here as in all aspects of teen-age life, ought to be that the rules must be clearly outlined by adults, strictly enforced by home and school, and the teen-age access to the car regarded as a privilege, not a birthright.

6 *Mass Media: Assembly-Line Idols*

It is through the mass media that the images and desires of teen-agers are at once standardized and distorted. The printed word, the television screen, the movies and that no man's land between art and entertainment—the record industry—simultaneously extract the flashiest, most obscene and least meaningful aspects of adolescence and crystallize this titillating mixture into a commercial formula which is then beamed at teen-age America.

Violence and frenzy—substitutes for real action and motion—are always present either as the main theme or leitmotif. The family, if it is not actually in a state of total disintegration, is never free from open or thinly camouflaged hostility. Father is usually portrayed as an ineffective but often lovable bungler, though occasionally he can be held responsible for all the town's—and the world's—ills. In the theater, the comic and heart-warming growing pains of *Junior Miss* have given way to the misunderstood youth-in-trouble of *Blue Denim.* In the movies there is the parent-persecuted immaturity of *Splendor in the Grass.* In literature, the adventurous Tom Sawyer has been replaced by the lost and unloved Holden Caulfield of *Catcher in the Rye.* Instead of drifting down a lazy river, teen-agers of modern literature drag-race down an aimless road of meaningless danger or get themselves senselessly beaten by a pimp in a flea-bag hotel.

Many of today's plots stress victory without effort, except for brief flashes of violence. Instead of the worship of heroes who have triumphed after long labors and privations, the modern teen-age idols win with a punch in the nose.

"Think of the Count of Monte Cristo's years in jail, his suffering, his incredible patience, and the industry and study of the abbé's teaching; both his gain and his vengeance are moralized by these prolongations, and he is an old man when, after many chapters, he wins," writes David Riesman. Then he adds: "By contrast, the comic-book or radio-drama hero wins almost effortlessly; the very curtailment of the telling time itself makes this more apparent." By foreshortening, the story itself and the lesson it tries to teach become unimportant, if not nonexistent. The adolescent, says Riesman, is increasingly prepared "for the adult role of betting on the right horse, with no interest in the jockey or horse or the knowledge of what it takes to be either. The content of the identification is impoverished to the point where virtually the only bond between reader and hero is the fact that the hero is winning."

Today's mass heroes are concrete creations. They are drawn in the comic strips or pictures on the screen. They leave nothing to the imagination. They come ready-made, look the same to all youngsters, and permit no personal embellishment. If young people want to "identify" with them, they must "adjust" to the unchangeable image as it is. There are no escape hatches for flights of fancy. The invisible Tinker Bell has been replaced by a standardized, uniformed Superman.

"Exposed to ever more sophisticated media, the children are too hep for 'unrealistic' daydreams," says Riesman. "At the movies they soon learn the fine points and will criticize a Western because the hero fired seven shots running from his six-shooter."

Hero worship is an important part of adolescence. Youngsters grow up with models of manhood or womanhood in their minds. Their goals, aspirations and behavior are constantly influenced by these models.

What are today's teen-age heroes really like?

The most important common denominator of most teen-age idols is that they are mass-produced. They are not really people, with individual characteristics and personalities: they appear to have been made in a mold. They are managed. They are "handled" commercially. They did not grow; they were manufactured by press agents, publicity departments and the vast and efficient machinery of public relations. Their success story is told almost entirely by dollar signs, Cadillacs and swimming pools. They share with teen-agers a semiliterate jargon and an almost total absence of original ideas. Yet, in an obscenely labored way, they strive to be "wholesome." They love "Mom and Dad" and moon over childhood sweethearts turned child brides.

A look at the actual image of the idols created by what

may well be the most important of the mass media, the record industry of the Rock 'n' Roll era and, more recently, the Twist, will illustrate the point.

Elvis Presley has been an idol longest. In his late twenties, he is a veteran who has inspired teen-agers for over five years. It seems a long time since his gyrations—he was known as Elvis the Pelvis then—outraged some viewers and threatened to turn his appearance on the Ed Sullivan Show into a national controversy. The solution then was to have the cameras concentrate on the singer only from the waist up. (In passing, it might be added that the teen-age influence has been strong and persistent enough to make the Twist not only a housebroken exhibition but actually a public pastime not only of adults but of high society.)

Presley was pushed to fame and fortune by his hips and his mentor, Colonel Tom Parker. After "Heartbreak Hotel," his first record, the way was paved by suggestive pseudo notoriety, swooning nymphette starlets, hysterical fan clubs, superb press-agentry (which followed him through the army and hints of romance with German teen-agers) and finally led to the movies. It is the pattern of patterns.

Today he is a hot property, guarded by a hand-picked group of young companions who act out the rat-pack mixture of clique and bodyguard. They live and work with him and fill the two Cadillacs which are his inevitable means of transportation. The coterie commutes with Elvis between the studio and his carefully guarded estate. When he decides to patronize a night club advance notice is given, apparently for combined reasons of safety and publicity. Like royalty, he is said never to carry cash.

The other side of the image, equally standard for successful teen-idols, is the impression of the dazed country boy—or, more specifically, in the Presley instance, the truck driver. At this point, messy sentimentality and the vulgarity of the *nouveau riche* become hopelessly mixed. Presley, we learn, keeps his pink Cadillac because it was Mom's favorite. Occasionally, like the daring heroes of the soap operas, he is given to musings about the "fundamentals." At such moments he flexes his muscles and says that someday, if fame should prove fleeting, he could always return to the honest labor of driving a truck.

To an outsider, the list of idols seems staggering. A partial listing of the "singers" currently popular includes Bobby Rydell, Frankie Avalon, Tommy Sands (married to Frank

Sinatra's daughter, Nancy), Bobby Vee, Pat Boone, Rick Nelson, Fabian, Bobby Darin, Paul Anka and Duane Eddy. By the innocent non-teen listener, the performers of Rock 'n' Roll cannot be told apart unless they are specifically identified. Teen-agers seem to identify their heroes mainly by the songs with which each is linked. But to the uninitiated, most of these singers appear to be the product of an assembly line, as interchangeable as the packages of detergents in the supermarket. They not only sound alike, they look alike as well, partly because of the standardization of their mannerisms. The non-teen-ager, when looking at a picture of one of the Bobbys must think hard before he can tell whether the last name is Darin, Vee or Rydell. The heavy, brooding, fleshy faces wear the mask of the same disgruntlement. Most of the young men seem to be short and slightly pudgy. Many of them have been "fixed up" with "nose jobs," contact lenses, elaborate hairdos and rigorous diets, in a manner that used to be reserved for aspiring starlets in their attempts to achieve whatever "look" was currently fashionable.

By the same token, the song "delivery" is so well established, defined and standardized that it has become frozen into a tribal ritual rather than an art form. It is not at all startling to show-biz experts that many of these "singers" cannot sing in public because they have been literally put together by and on tape. Their records consist of elaborate splicings of tape to eliminate mistakes. Lack of natural volume in their voices is overcome by the "echo chamber," which gives their recorded songs not only a petulantly wailing and barely comprehensible quality but makes them sound as though they were singing in a fish tank.

In many instances lack of real talent is so complete an obstacle to any personal performance in public that the young "artist" just mouths the words and hopes that the public-address system which carries his pre-recorded voice will not break down. This novel form of "singing" in public is known in the trade as "lip sync." It is the serious counterpart of one of the oldest vaudeville comedy acts—and it is not intended to be funny. Its purpose is to eliminate talent as a prerequisite for the performing arts.

While not all teen singers use this extreme technique for "legitimate" deception, most of them rely on accompanying tricks and gestures to put their songs over and make the audience judge and love them for reasons other than their mournfully synthetic voices. Never has the public been given such a variety of swaying, hip-swinging and, of course, the inevitable finger-snapping. These mannerisms are frequently the only "comprehensible" part of a performance which puts a premium on unintelligible diction.

Because the heroes worshiped by adolescents inevitably color their young admirers' ideas and ideals, they cannot help but influence the teen-agers' concept of the qualities needed to rise to fame and fortune.

The only thing these modern heroes have in common with the old Horatio Alger legends, however, is that most of them did start as poor boys who wanted to make good. Few, if any, of them thought of themselves as singers or had any strong urge to excel as artists. Popular singing simply seemed the quickest and easiest road to the financial top. And the road is lined with instant glamour.

Almost invariably, the search for success starts with the preliminary search for a manager. Behind almost every teen-age millionaire is that modern Miracle Man—the agent. Usually, an older man, wise in the ways of press-agentry, manipulation of fan clubs, the do's and don'ts of disc-jockeying for position, contacts with celebrities and gossip columnists and expertise with booking agents, is to be credited with the creation of the manufactured idols. Elvis Presley has his Colonel Parker, Fabian has Bob Marcucci, Bobby Darin has Steve Blauner, Paul Anka has Irvin Feld. The modern road to success is paved with good introductions. It is a road with predictable traffic regulations.

Any disagreement or rumor of a potential "split" between a singer and his manager assumes all the overtones of divorce proceedings among Hollywood stars.

The now well-traveled road to teen fame and fortune leads through the phases of disc-jockey praises, guest performances and personal appearances in the plush adult saloons and night clubs, such as the Copacabana in New York, or the Sands in Las Vegas. High-rated TV shows are, of course, the utlimate goal. At this point, teen-age and adult paths join, and it is here, along with the teen-age domination of the radio, that the depressing abdication of adult taste to teen-age ways is most apparent.

Not unaware of the power of the teen-age market, adult stars, add their effusive praise to the press releases and the album covers. Featured prominently, for instance, on a Darin album is a telegram from Sammy Davis, Jr.: "Dear Bobby, Have just heard the dubs for your new Album. What can I say? They're so good I hate you. But seriously, Bobby, I think the album's another step in a career that I feel will last a long time. I anxiously await public's reaction to the album in this day and age of gimmick sounds and gimmick records . . . a perfect combination of showmanship, performance, and taste. In other words, I dig it, see you soon."

The next step is the movies. As Paul Anka has been quoted: "Movies. That's where the real loot is."

Since modern teen-age idols are clearly in pursuit of art for loot's sake (perhaps nothing more sinister than a reflection of the more general values of society), it is pertinent to ask about the way of life to which the loot leads. It is after all, inevitable that the adolescents' heroes, by the way they live and the things they value, influence the aspirations of their admirers.

Except for Bobby Darin, who is married, most of the idols are required to live fairly secluded private lives. The story is told that Paul Anka, when he was performing at the Steel Pier in Atlantic City, looked at people on the boardwalk through a telescope. "This is as close as I can get," he said, "without two cops watching me."

Anka gets an "allowance" and lives in New Jersey in a beautiful house, shared with his father, younger brother and sister. The allowance plays an important part in the publicity stories about the teen-idols. It appears to form the personal-identification link between hero and worshiper.

Frankie Avalon, according to the press-agent biographers, is a perfect example of this mingling of big business profits and teen-age jargon. Chancellor Records, owned by his managers Bob Marcucci and Pete De Angelis, was reported to have grossed more than $2,000,000 in 1960, less than five years after its establishment. When Frankie turned twenty-one, he recalls, "The first thing I did when I came into my money was to increase my allowance. I had been getting thirty-five dollars a week. Now I give myself enough so that I can go out on a date and not worry about blowing all my allowance in one night, then be broke the rest of the week."

In this no man's land between teen-terms and millionaire life, how does an idol with a thirty-five-dollar "allowance" actually live? *Photoplay* magazine describes a visit to the Avalon home in a New Jersey suburb. The closets in the

$100,000 house are filled with nostalgic mementoes of less affluent days. Frankie built his house, we are told (in the standard terms of the sentimental legend), not for himself but for Mom and Dad, who are treated with a mixture of mushy love and the condescension of a successful younger generation toward its simple-minded elders. "The first night they were here, they didn't sleep a wink—they stayed up to play with the light switches and try out the gadgets." The child describes with amused indulgence the wonder of discovery on the part of poor parents. This, in test-tube exaggeration, is a reflection of the awe with which too many of today's parents hold the sophistication (no matter how pseudo) of their adolescent children.

With the instinct of a *nouveau riche* culture, Frankie said: "Sure I told an interviewer what this house costs. He asked me . . . and I told him. I wasn't crowing or sounding off . . . I bought it for my folks, my Mom and Dad."

Then the unintentioned parody becomes broad satire. "There goes Pop," Frankie is quoted. "A regular hot-rodder. . . . Dad's never had a Cadillac and he always wanted one. He always says, 'There's nothing like a Cadi.' So, as a present to myself, for the kicks I'll get when I see his face, I'm going to buy him one for my birthday."

Here is the perfect formula for the modern teen-age fairy tale, with its solemn reversal of traditional roles, much as in the more normal childish games in which the little girl becomes the mother. The teen-age idol, posing as a typical teen-ager, complete with allowance, describes the happy glow as he lets the poor, underprivileged, immature parent have his toy, the Cadi he always wanted.

And what of the house of the successful teen-ager with the thirty-five-dollar allowance? It is a big, sprawling red-brick ranch with imported marble floor and sunken living room. It has thirteen rooms, four baths, a music room and a trophy room. Frankie's bedroom has a spiral staircase which leads directly down to the private swimming pool. It's a long way from the log cabin heroes of simpler days.

Today's adults, in their thirties and forties, may look back at the beginning of Frank Sinatra's career, with its headlines about swooning bobby-soxers, and ask: "What's so different now?"

Sinatra was, of course, among the first of the singers to be discovered by teen-agers and to grow up to be an adult performer. But there is a difference. First of all, Sinatra could sing. He had real talent that was not created by mechanical devices. His career today, though by no means harmed by publicity and press-agentry, is based on proven ability as a crooner and, since his role in *From Here to Eternity,* as an actor, as well.

In the early forties psychiatrists said that Sinatra came along just at the right time, during the war years when men were scarce and war fears had shattered women's nerves. They called Frankie the "love object" of girls suffering from real or imagined war loneliness. They said that the skinny singer appealed to women's maternal instincts. Whatever the reasons, there could be no doubt about his potent effects. Ushers at the Paramount Theater where he sang had to carry smelling salts in order to revive swooning females.

The real trouble is that while the prerequisite of talent appears to have been dropped, the worst aspects of the Sinatra phenomenon seem to have survived. (In all fairness, it should be added that there is, of course, even today some real talent among the teen-age singers. Pat Boone does sing and knows how. He even completed college, having graduated with honors from Columbia.)

Critic Dwight MacDonald, writing for the *New Yorker,* explained the progressive worsening of symptoms, like the early Sinatra craze transferred to successors without either his talent or his originality, as a kind of chain reaction. "Like the dancing mania of the Middle Ages, this sort of movement is self-expanding," he says. "The more it seems that 'everybody' is doing a thing, the more everybody feels he must do it."

Ernest Hemingway has described the present age as the Millennium of the Untalented. He said: "We are deluged with writers who can't write, actors who can't act and singers who can't sing—and they are all making a million dollars a year." This is borne out in the field of popular music.

Other than the sheer power of press-agentry, what are some of the possible reasons for the rise of the untalented? Mitch Miller calls Rock 'n' Roll the musical baby food. "The kids don't want recognized stars doing *their* music," he believes. "They don't want real professionals. They want faceless young people doing it in order to retain the feeling that it is their own." This comes close to Dwight MacDonald's diagnosis: "Here [in the Rock 'n' Roll music] one may observe in its purest form the teen-agers' defiance of adult control, their dominance of certain markets, their tendency to set themselves up as a caste and the tribal rituals and special dialects they have evolved."

A Swiss psychologist speaks of the adolescents' general need for a conception of life that permits self-assertion and the creation of something new that is their own. By default, Rock 'n' Roll fills the bill. And at the same time, it is an indication of the adult failure to offer a better focus for the adolescents' creative interests.

This becomes doubly serious when adults not only condone but adopt the teen-age culture. Teen-idols have become the heroes of Café Society and the stars of the night clubs where the gossip columnists are foreign correspondents reporting from the world of the busy *nouveau riche* to the rest of America. Charles Laufer, editor of *Teen Magazine,* said (with some exaggeration which needs to be discounted but not disallowed): "The music market for the first time in history is completely dominated by the young set." If the word "dominated" is replaced with "seriously infiltrated and influenced," then there can be no question about the effect of teen-age influences on American taste.

A psychiatrist puts it this way: "Today . . . we have a society in America that tends toward infantilism. With the uncertainties of the world being what they are, we have a compulsive desire to go back to the simple existence of childhood. How do we do this? Through adopting for ourselves the tastes and pleasures of children. By working through our young, therefore, clever opportunists can sell us anything. That's why television, for instance, is loaded with crime and Westerns and situation-comedy shows of the quality of the comic strips we read when we were kids. The children like them, and in an attempt to escape back to childhood, we like them."

The success of the Twist is a flagrant example of a teen-age fad dominating the adult world. The forces of adolescent culture, publicity, mass communications and—the ultimate stamp of mass approval—New York's Café Society, with its mixture of synthetic socialites and decadent aristocracy (domestic and imported), have combined to spread the fad from an obscure teen-age pastime via an even more obscure bar and dance saloon, the Peppermint Lounge, to suburban and society dinner parties.

It serves as a case par excellence. The Twist's origins are obscure. It is said to have grown out of a dance called the Madison which originated in Philadelphia and was based on Rock 'n' Roll music. Partners shake their shoulders, swing their hips in synchronized motion toward each other but without touching. It has the elements of bump-and-grind exhibitionism on an amateur level.

Nineteen-year-old Chubby Checker and twenty-two-year-old Joey Dee are often considered the fathers of the Twist. By now it's teen-age beginnings are only a faint memory. While socialites and teen-agers patiently stood in line to gain admission to the Peppermint Lounge, Mr. Dee, its band leader, was inundated with invitations to play at posh parties and dinners. His quintet was asked to play at the expensive Four Seasons restaurant to raise money for Girls Town, thus putting adult exhibitionism in the front lines of the fight against juvenile delinquency. Later, the Twist King entertained at Mayor Wagner's victory ball at the Astor Hotel.

Probably the summit of success came for Joey Dee when he was asked to play at the fashion industry's Party of the Year, a one-hundred-dollar-a-plate dinner held appropriately at the Metropolitan Museum of Art for the benefit of the museum's Costume Institute. Beside the serene pool and the classic columns, in the shrine of Rembrandt, New York's fashionable adults twisted to the tune of "You Can't Sit Down." And although it was reported that the museum's director "shook with dismay" when he discovered what was going on, *New York Times* reporter Gay Talese wrote: "Members of Café Society approached Joey Dee with reverence, and one imperial gentleman, straight-spined in a tuxedo, hesitated before asking, 'Joey, may I please have your autograph?' Many others begged Joey Dee to continue his music, even if it meant holding up the rest of the show, which included dinner and a parade of historic costumes from the museum's collection."

Chic *Vogue* magazine joined the procession and adorned an issue with glossy pictures of debutantes doing the Twist in elegant night clubs. One of its editors, unaccustomed to such earthy language and motion, was trying to learn the proper body movements. She was told by "a duck-tailed teen-age bystander: 'You gotta feel it, honey.' "

As might be expected, the Twist had its commercial repercussions in the record industry. *Billboard* magazine reported one of the most unusual turnabouts in the business. About a year and a half before the fall of 1961 (the height of the Twist), there had been made a "sub-teen" or single record called "The Twist" which had reached the Number One spot on *Billboard*'s "Hot 100" and then spiraled down and out in the usual manner. But by January 1961, the same record had made it to the top spot a second time, its return performance the result of the adult craze. The adults had taken over where the sub-teens left off according to *Billboard's* research director, a "first" in the record market.

Consequently at the end of 1961, Twist records, sold in albums rather than as singles which are generally aimed at the teen market, were considered a stronghold of the adult trade. If some of those adults who buy the Twist records have a taste for the ironic, they might muse about the Rock 'n' Roll transformation of the lovely tune from *My Fair Lady* into groans of "I coulda, coulda, coulda danced a-all night," in what might be described as a Pygmalion-in-reverse. Eliza, along with teen-jargoned American adulthood, appears headed back to illiterate vulgarity.

By January 1961, four of the ten best-selling albums were of the Twist, topped only by Elvis Presley and Mitch Miller.

Students of American fads meanwhile have been hard at work trying to explain the popularity of the Twist among adults, in an attempt to get a better insight into the growing pattern-setting tendency of teen-age behavior. Among the reasons cited is the desire to be young again by imitating what youth is doing, plus an old favorite used to explain away all inexplicable aberrations: the release of tensions in troubled times. Everybody is, of course, privileged to add his own theories. Those who are determined to find silver linings in every cloud of questionable taste, interpret Noel Coward and foreign nobility rubbing elbows or knees with duck-tailed teen-agers as a sign of disappearing social barriers and class differences. Psychiatrists are more likely to point to the primitive exhibitionist aspects of the dance. Earl Blackwell, publisher of Celebrity Register and himself a devotee of the Twist, attributes its popularity to another lure: "It's an easy dance to do. Everyone can do it." (Thus it is unusually suited for the Age of the Untalented. But doctors don't agree that overgrown and out-of-condition adult teen-agers should do the Twist. A Buffalo physician disclosed that knee injuries, generally considered an occupational hazard for football players, have become an epidemic. Ironically, the Heart Association's bulletin reported that this organization used a Twist party for adults and children for a benefit, thus potentially substituting a new disease in fighting an old one.)

Whatever the deep psychological reasons, the example of the Twist and its history points up the new trend of society: instead of youth growing up, adults are sliding down.

This need not be considered a matter for speculation. Chubby Checker, the originator of the Twist, explained it all succinctly in a brief article, "How Adults Stole the Twist," for *Datebook* magazine. He wrote:

"The Twist craze took me by surprise. It seems to me a long time ago that I first performed the dance at record hops around the country for teen-agers. I could see that the kids loved it. But, I was really dumbfounded when I found the adults doing the Twist later on, too. That's the way a lot of teen fads seem to develop though. First, the coolest kids take it up and then the rest of the young crowd follows. Very often, at the same time, the adults are finding fault and objecting for various reasons. But, then, the thing gets too big to be held back and it spreads right through the population, including every age group."

Mr. Checker accurately recalls that adults used to call Elvis Presley's gyrations vulgar. They even tried to get them banned.

"But right now, I bet you there are more adults numbered among Elvis' fans than there are teen-agers," he continues, and he may well have a winning bet on his hands. Therefore:

"Just give them enough time, I say, and you can win them over."

It would be hard to state the theory of creeping adult adolescence more simply, accurately and frighteningly.

What makes the adult acceptance of teen-cultural taste even more dismal is that most sociologists agree: the no-talent fare of the Rock 'n' Roll class is accepted only by the low- and middle-brow mass of the teen-agers but not by the teen-age elite. Sociologist James S. Coleman points out in *The Adolescent Society* that, instead of being most tuned in to the mass-produced popular music, the "leaders of the adolescent culture" are the least interested in Rock 'n' Roll music and the adolescent heroes like Elvis Presley. A Baltimore teen-age girl, quoted in the same book, typically stresses that "among the elites . . . there is no swooning over R 'n' R singers. It is the drapettes and the unaccepted girls who are in fan clubs and swoon over these singers."

In other words, the adults who are adopting adolescent tastes are succumbing to the adolescent low rather than high life.

7 *TV: Armchair Thrills*

A television series, called *Bus Stop,* created considerable nationwide comment when it widely advertised the appearance of teen-age singer-idol, Fabian, as the star in one of the worst episodes of sex and sadism ever to hit the home screen. In the course of this "family" drama, the young hoodlum (portrayed by Fabian) senselessly kills an innocent old shopkeeper, becomes entangled with the alcoholic wife of the District Attorney, pulls a switchblade on another teenager whose girl he is trying to take away, lies and bullies himself through a court session, tries to shake down a budding young Lolita (who had flung herself at him in a manner which might appear forward to Brigitte Bardot) and quickly abandons her when she appears of no financial use to him. Finally, he murders in cold blood the lawyer who had been defending him and had saved his life. In an apparent psychological aside he accompanies some of his worst outrages with a crooning rendition of a song called "Couldn't Hear Nobody Pray."

As an exhibition of the psychotic killer this was par for television's course of family fare. Combined with the idiom and mannerisms of the teen-age idol, the total effect was obscene. In addition, the apparent submission of the TV adults to the disrespect of the young hood was a reflection of the helplessness that has grown out of the concept of permissive handling of adolescents. Thus, when Fabian keeps his feet on the table during cross-examination, when he swaggers and leers his way through an extended courtroom scene, when he insolently insists on calling the District Attorney "Poppa Bear" and his pathetic wife "Mother Goose," when he refers to justice as "the lady with the blindfold," none of his elders, some of them quite obviously the pillars of society and the protectors of law and order, have the courage or good sense to talk to him via a good beating, the language he appears to understand. Nobody even calls him to order.

Nor was the portrayal of the other teen-agers, seen in a dance joint amid highballs and low leers, very encouraging. Even though Fabian had brutally attacked one of the "regulars," the girls appear ready to throw themselves at him, and the entire teen-age crowd cheers wildly when the insolent hood manages to hoodwink the law and "gets off."

A Lion Walks Among Us, as the show was called, admittedly set something of a record in violence and obscenity. It was also quite blatantly an attempt by adults to exploit, for sensational and commercial purposes, the worst aberrations of adolescent society—and do it through an acknowledged hero of that society. Fortunately, there were strong signs that the better instincts of adult America are healthy enough to call a halt to such excesses. Many television stations canceled the show as unsuitable for family entertainment. A Cincinnati television executive said: "As a result of the hue and cry in advance of the show we asked the network for a screening. After previewing the program, we decided to cancel it on our stations."

Perhaps as good an indication as any that these precautions were not out of place was a phone call to the *New York Times* by a fifteen-year-old girl from a New York suburb in protest against unfavorable reviews given the Fabian show. She said she "had made a survey among the kids in school and we all thought it was wonderful."

Why do teen-agers like violence, crime and filth on television? Dr. George Gallup diagnosed it as a kind of escape from the unpleasantness of reality by making unpleasantness itself a spectator sport.

"I don't think I could stand those kind of men who spit and curse and do bad things. I don't want to see the raws of life in the flesh," was a typical reply.

"With television," one youngster explained, "you're not involved. You can always turn it off if it gets too dreadful—and it never does. And when there's torture or killing or poverty, you don't feel the pain. Then when it's over, you can get a glass of milk and a sandwich, and everything's okay again. You get adventure, but no risk." It is a form of slumming without getting one's feet dirty and one's mind too upset. Like everything else, the thrills come packaged.

Television, in other words, gives teen-agers comfortable adventure and vicarious violence, neatly wrapped in celluloid with an electronic buffer against excessive scruples.

But television does more. It reflects and, at the same time, reinforces an image of the American family whose message cannot be lost on the average teen-ager. Gone are the days of the wise and knowing father of even so saccharine a serial as *Andy Hardy*. In his stead, we find with predictable regularity the amiable boob of the situation comedies. He is an endless variation of the all-American theme of Dagwood Bumpstead, the ineffectual but lovable bungler. He needs constantly to be saved from his feeble-minded aimiability (which, however, rarely seems to interfere with his ability to supply his family with the cash to keep up with the Joneses, with whose breadwinner he frequently joins in hilariously inane ventures).

On a fairly typical Tom Ewell show, the hard-pressed and, as always, slightly imbecile father is hit for five dollars by the bright-eyed, pony-tailed teen-age daughter who "must" have a man's shirt because this has been proclaimed the required uniform for the class dance. Daddy cheerfully offers one of his shirts but is told that only a new one will do. When he protests, a teen-understanding mother comes to the defense of teen-law. "Do you want her to be different from all the others?" she asks. Dad, by now properly humbled and ashamed, shells out the cash.

The national P.T.A. magazine describes all family situation-comedy shows with the collective title, "The Queen in the Kitchen," to underline the standard story line.

"The family is a matriarchy, the mother governing with an iron hand gloved in an attitude of amused tolerance," the magazine says. "Perfectly groomed, petite, piquant, and petulant, she floats with the greatest of ease through family crises and kitchen chores. . . . The Queen often makes mistakes, but she never learns. Each new situation is approached with the same flippant complacency. The muddle-headed family, including the cipher who goes by the name of Dad, usually comes meekly to heel."

Howard Taubman, *New York Times* drama critic, reviewing the Broadway play, *Take Her, She's Mine,* which portrays a father of a college girl, has this to say about the inevitable characterization of Dad: "He is loving, eager, naïve and sentimental, like nearly all the nebulous fathers one encounters in films and on television. Although the play mutes the wisdom of Mom, the inevitable concomitant in such fictions, it conforms. Mrs. M. does not say much, but she knows best. It's the sweet, familiar, corny American dream."

It might be said that there is some earlier precedent for the boob-image of the American father. Even in such a classic as *Life With Father* it was perfectly clear to the audience that Mother Vinnie really ran the family and always got her way. But there still was, despite this unmistakable germ of Momism, a difference. It was always made to appear that Father was the ultimate authority. No matter how elaborate the subterfuges, the strong image of the father was upheld. In that early stage of the domination by Mother, appearances were still kept. Today, by contrast, there is an overt and cheerful acceptance of Dad's decline. Even the shaggy little dog knows. But while a hasty glimpse might lead the viewer to believe that Mom is wearing the pants, she is merely the caretaker and spokesman for the real power behind the throne—the children.

Television, especially in its day-to-day bread-and-butter programing, has adopted so many of the teen-age standards that it is hard to keep adolescent and adult shows apart. What possible excuse, for instance, is there for a general airing of a show such as the *American Bandstand* which features teen-age exhibitionists dancing past the cameras? What legitimate pleasure could be derived from the spectacle of duck- and pony-tailed youngsters gyrating for the benefit of the American public?

Perhaps underlining the point made earlier by Coleman that the teen-age elite happily disdains the worst of the teen-age crooner-idols, while the mass of American adults appear to succumb to the tastes of the lowbrow teens, columnist John Crosby wrote about television: "In America, no responsible people look at television. And by nobody, I mean nobody—no clergy, no senators, nobody. Nobody but people. When you have a vast conglomeration of leaderless people, you have a mob. And when you have a mob, the best place to aim is the groin—which is exactly where most of the high-rated television shows aim."

Crosby's point is that the vast outpouring of television does not get any critical attention at all. The late John Lardner, he adds, was the only major reviewer who occasionally analyzed the regular, everyday television fare which is so intimately related to teen-age tastes and which, in a continuing vicious circle, steadily reaches the teen-age audience.

More recently, the national magazine of the Congress of Parents and Teachers has entered the field of TV criticism and, incidentally, is doing a hard-hitting, intelligent and unsparing job.

This is encouraging, especially since the intellectual community has been of so little help in putting television in the proper perspective. The intellectual snob has, from the start, ignored the advent of the new medium. To say, "I never watch," is still considered a declaration of intellectual class at most highbrow cocktail parties. This is another abdication of responsibility and a refusal to take part in contemporary culture. It is an additional step on the dangerous road of letting adolescent society and immature tastes set the standards for mass communications.

8 *The Movies: Through Technicolored Glasses*

It is hard to tell which has greater impact on the manners and tastes of teen-agers—the Hollywood product or the teen-age Hollywood way of life.

In the movies themselves, the adult, responsible, sometimes tough and sometimes tender man (personified in the past by Clark Gable or Spencer Tracy) is increasingly replaced by the child-man, sensitive only to his own problems. Often this sulking hero exudes spoiled selfishness, maudlin self-pity and a strong dose of self-destruction. He is a crazy mixed-up kid, but it is always made abundantly clear that his problems have been forced on him by a hostile society, a weakling father, a broken home and other outside forces.

As for the Hollywood way of teen-age life, perhaps the best monument to the image itself is the tragic death of teen-age idol James Dean in a sports car accident. With the help of the mass media, teen-agers turned the funeral into an orgy of mourning, and the star's fame rose to greater heights after his death than he had achieved during his short lifetime. The volume of his posthumous fan mail—a strange exercise in youthful necrophilia—kept rising. There were at least three television programs modeled after his life, plus numerous cover stories in mass circulation magazines. The movie fan magazines, edited largely for teen-agers and adults with permanently teen-age minds, had a field day of maudlin morbidity, not exhibited since the days of Rudolph Valentino.

In his two successful movies, *Rebel Without a Cause* and *East of Eden,* James Dean established (with far greater real talent than many of his imitators since then) the pattern of the teen-age movie "hero." He is a petulant boy, skirting the brink of delinquency, son of a father who is either too weak to be of any use or simply "doesn't understand."

During most of the running-time the "hero" has a chip on his shoulder. He acts alternatingly out of weakness and truculence. To conform to the "happy ending" formula he stresses reform, if not basic, deep-down goodness at the end; but the real impact glorifies the antisocial behavior of rudderless adolescents in a chaotic or ridiculous adult world.

Dwight MacDonald describes the teen-ager in the movies and the movie influence on the teen-ager: "The movies present the teen-ager as sinister but exciting—and an image is built up that in most cases merely compels him to behave rudely at breakfast, but in others tempts him to go in for more sensational misdeeds, preferably in bad company.... Mischief is always attractive to a child.... When mischief can be pursued with others as part of a recognized movement, it becomes even more seductive."

A classic example is the durable, sulking Marlon Brando as the leader of a group of cyclists who terrorize an entire town in *The Wild One*. His image is reflected on city streets, in high school corridors and subways. He is the unkempt but cocklike, overcombed, sallow youth, dressed in black leather jacket, the uniform of the adolescent mob. His speech is the inarticulate, monosyllabic accompaniment to the awkward gestures and the phony swagger which convey arrogance without backbone.

Another disturbing reflection of the changed status of the teen-ager in society is the treatment of teen-age romance in what is offered as adult entertainment, but cannot help but have its effect on adolescents as well. *Spendor in the Grass*, William Inge's first original screenplay, has transferred the conflict between physical craving and the desire for chastity from the arena of young adulthood to the high school scene. The playwright is not to blame; he reflects the faster growing up of teen-age bodies, unaccompanied by the maturing of their minds, which has been the carefully promoted tragedy of today's adolescent culture. If the Inge theme were not so serious (and so perceptively written), it might almost be taken to be parody. All the stock problems and figures of the human tragedy have been reduced in age to create a teen-age version of *Kitty Foyle*. The wealthy teen-age boy is told by his gross and crass father not to get himself involved with the nice girl from the wrong side of the tracks but to find himself a satisfactory but safe woman to sleep with. Just the advice that in earlier fiction might have been given under similar circumstances to the young man in college! By the same token, the anxious mother of the poor high school girl would like nothing better than a "good" match—the earlier the better. Even the *femme fatale* to whom the boy turns, driven partly by his girl's virtue and his father's counsel, is no longer the traditional older and experienced woman of an earlier age of truth and fiction; it is the class tramp of the comprehensive co-educational high school. Mr. Inge does not hold a brief for the pitiful, motorized adolescent immaturity of *Splendor in the Grass*. On the contrary, he sees it leading (through temporary insanity) to a frighteningly ordinary, dull, unsatisfactory and unromantic adult life, with children underfoot and the necessary appliances in the kitchen.

On the lighter, hearts-and-flowers side, *Come September* offers an example of the Hollywood product aimed at both teens and their elders. It stars Old Folks, Gina Lollobrigida and Rock Hudson, and Young Folks, Sandra Dee and Bobby Darin. American millionaire Hudson checks in two months too early for his annual visit to his Italian villa and mistress. The villa has been turned, without his knowledge, into a resort hotel inhabited at the time by a group of American teen-age girls, including Sandra, and beleaguered by some anxious teen-age males.

In an early scene, Sandra barges into Rock Hudson's room and gets him to relax on a couch merely to apply her knowledge of freshman psychology. After hasty analysis of the grown man by the adolescent girl, the man is given—and accepts—the child's prescription.

Throughout, Rock Hudson sternly lectures and avidly protects the girls' chastity while madly pursuing his mistress. The rest of the plot appears to follow the standard line of so many of the advice books for teen-agers: encourage a maximum of romance with a minimum of sex, a national fiction which has made the teen-agers' social life increasingly difficult, unsatisfactory and schizophrenic. Perhaps this is what *Seventeen* magazine had in mind when, in a review of the picture, it concluded: "None of this make-believe is to be taken seriously, but some of it will be too broad for a younger sister." This may be a crucial warning, lest Mr. Inge will, in the not too distant future, have to look for his *femmes fatales* in the nation's elementary schools.

In addition to what might be termed adult teen-age movies

(the counterpart of adult Westerns), Hollywood turns out scores of films made unmistakably for the pony-tail set. These are low-budget, high-income pictures in which adults are not really expected to show any interest. The teen market promises to be satisfactory, without grown-up support.

Perhaps "crazy mixed-up pictures" is the only proper description for most of these irrelevant movies. Like many of the youngsters in the audience, the stories and the characterizations simply have no direction. As Dwight MacDonald puts it: "It is never clear how the audience is supposed to feel about the dramatis personae, since everybody, admirable or despicable, behaves the same—tough, sexy, jive-talking and generally hopped-up. This ambiguity may reflect the teen-ager's own confusion as to whether he's a Good Guy or a Bad Guy—or, more exciting and romantic, both at the same time. [It may also reflect a low level of screenwriting, where the scenarist just doesn't know how to change dialog.] It certainly reflects the instinct of Hollywood to have it both ways, pleasing the P.T.A. as well as the problem child."

Actually, it is doubtful that P.T.A. members ever look at these films or that Hollywood wants their box-office business. As things are, it costs relatively little to produce a typical teen-age class ("C minus") picture and it is considered quite normal for such formula-built products to earn spectacular profits.

The titles themselves give a fair idea of this art form. There are such movies as *Juvenile Jungle, Live Fast, Die Young, High School Confidential, Rock Around the Clock, The Explosive Generation* and *Teen-Age Millionaire*. By way of random example, the "hero" of *High School Confidential* acts just like any villain or overgrown juvenile delinquent. He uses a switchblade knife, the badge of manhood among the teen hoodlums. He pushes dope in the locker room. But in the last reel, all turns out well because our "hero" was—working for the F.B.I. all the time. What better way of eating your thrills and having your virtue intact, too?

In all fairness, *The Explosive Generation* is considerably above the average teen-age movie. It tries to come to grips with some of the problems which worry teen-agers and adults alike, in this instance whether teen-age sex problems should be dealth with in the classrooms. (This is a perennial question in a society which gives adolescents a maximum of stimulus, mock maturity and romantic license, but expects everything to stop automatically at the danger point.) In the film, a sympathetic teacher understandingly sides with the students and is willing to discuss with them their perplexing sex problems. The community reacts with familiar Puritan ire, condemns the "sex survey," and suspends the teacher. In a mixture of soap opera and teen-age triumph, the youngsters have to go on strike before everybody can live happily ever after in the last reel.

Finally, there is the category of the teen-age horror films, a kind of mixture of celluloid comic strip and adolescent peep show. Among the titles are *I Was a Teen-Age Frankenstein* and *I Was a Teen-Age Werewolf.* In these movies, the real villain is always an adult mad scientist or his equivalent. The teen-ager is the helpless victim-medium who has no will of his own but kills and terrorizes at the command of an adult.

This formula permits adolescents to identify with the thrilling violence of the "victim-hero" and at the same time enjoy the superior knowledge of not really doing anything wrong. In a sense this acts out the fate-driven irresponsibility of the teen-ager who is "the product of his environment" or the "prisoner of the world created by his elders." It offers the combination package of the satisfaction of sinning and the confident peace of mind that comes from knowing that it is all somebody else's fault.

Since the teen-age Hollywood market place cannot afford to underestimate the power of the female clientele, *Blood of Dracula* makes its unwilling victim-villain-hero a sensitive young girl who has been sent to boarding school after her mother's death. (Dad, in the male boob tradition, has married an insensitive blonde tramp.) The teen-heroine falls under the spell of a wicked lady science teacher and acquires the remarkable capacity of sprouting fangs at the teacher's command.

It is hardly surprising that such aberrations, like any existing enterprise (especially if it is profitable), are being defended on the theory that they serve as harmless outlets for adolescent fears and fancies.

There is little in the shabbiness of these pictures to warrant so high-minded a defense, and it would be surprising indeed to find among their producers anyone who has these goals in mind. As for those who point to the traditional fairy tales and even to many of the specific stories of the Bible as being full of terror and violence, they forget that there the horror is merely part of a greater artistic creation, a description of man's place in a larger pattern. To equate terror in literature or in religion with the exploitation of horror in the screen's equivalent of pulp magazines is as dishonest as the defense of pornography on the theory that nudity can constitute great art. Altogether, there is little evidence that the great majority of films produced for the teen-age market are anything but exploitation of the worst adolescent tastes.

Inevitably, those tastes are influenced as much by the way teen-age Hollywood lives as by the Hollywood product itself. In many ways, adolescent movieland is like adolescent Main Street, only more so. Like the rest of the country's teenage set, that of the movie capital is a separate little world within a world.

Hollywood's junior grade has its own gossip, scandals and carriers-of-tales to those daily chroniclers of the oddities of life, the gossip columnists. The teen-age stars may not make quite as much money as their adult opposite numbers, and they face the added hazard that they may be through by the time they grow up, unless (as a few have proven to be possible) they can avoid growing up and remain in their teens for an extra decade or two.

Perhaps the quality that endears the teen-age stars most to the ordinary teen-agers is the carefully nurtured impression that they face the same problems and fears as the kids back home. Stress, therefore, is on the perennial soap-opera theme of how to find love and romance in spite of a six-figure income and how to manage meddling parents.

The Rock 'n' Roll stars largely solved their problem by supporting their parents economically in the style to which they thought the parents of successful teen-agers ought to become accustomed. Thus, they made the parents their dependents, an adolescent dream come true. Then, they substituted their managers for the lost adult authority, an acceptable solution because the managers technically can be exchanged for more understanding ones, if necessary. This cannot generally be done with parents.

Not all Hollywood teen-agers have been completely successful in working out this formula. In other words, they have had "typical" teen-age troubles. Sandra Dee and Bobby Darin, for instance, "had" to elope because her mother disapproved.

According to the fan magazines, which kept a running account of this story and thus offered hope and consolation to thousands of teen-agers with similar mother trouble, all turned out well, with a reconciliation between mother and daughter when the first baby arrived.

Tuesday Weld's running battles with her mother and other assorted adults are carefully kept in the headlines by her alert press agents. "Tuesday Weld and her mother are speaking again, but not living together," says a typical communiqué. "Tuesday barely missed sitting in hot water with the authorities by moving into her new home three weeks before her eighteenth birthday. Juvenile officers frown on girls living alone when they aren't of age."

How many teen-age fantasies are here rolled into one! A gracious but nonbinding reconciliation with mother; an independent life, not just in a cold-water, working girl's apartment but in a luxurious new home; and beating the nasty old "juvenile officers" in the bargain.

As for Tuesday's virtuosity as a teen-age philosopher and psychotherapist, she is a press agents' and fan magazines' dream. "The fact that I live with my mother," said Tuesday, carefully preparing the ground for moving out of the parent's bothersome reach, "a lot of times doesn't help matters because people criticize *her*. This makes her mad. She tries to stop me, and that makes it worse. She's always let me drink, though. She felt if a fruit was forbidden, it would be taken more quickly. But in other things she is not so tolerant."

Susan Barnes, a British newspaperwoman, during a visit to Hollywood, found Tuesday Weld "an unusual experience." In an article in the *New York World-Telegram and Sun*, Miss Barnes related some of the statements by the adolescent star which make her a favorite with the teen-age community across the country.

"I don't care about public opinion, but I do get tired of being nagged," she says in the prominent teen-ager's version of the ordinary adolescent's complaint that "I don't care what anybody says, but if only Mother would stop pestering me." The star continues: "It gets irritating. I shouldn't do this. I shouldn't do that. I shouldn't do anything. But I do. I just do it where people won't see me."

Here is the teen-age temper tantrum, placed on a national—no, even an international—stage.

Then there is the perfect child-psychological way out, whenever it is inconvenient to obey the rules. "If something is wrong," says this embodiment of teen-age daring, "I want to find out for myself. I don't want to take it on hearsay. Of course, this kind of attitude is hard on Mother.... But the time when I sit down and stop exploring, mentally as well as physically, I might as well be ten feet under. I don't think there's much sense in living if you're not going to do something you want to do."

Another young star named Deborah Walley, of *Gidget* fame, was shown in a fan magazine's picture spread, asking: "Mother, when does a girl become a woman?" The description that follows seems to draw the clear dividing line: the teen-ager spends hours in the bubble bath, talking on the phone and drinking chocolate sodas after skating in Central Park. But the emerging woman is shown in a backless black sheath dress to demonstrate that she is not really a teen-ager.

Possessions become a crucial yardstick, closely linked with everything, including romance and marriage. "I can change my clothes as much as fifteen or twenty times a day," boasts Tuesday Weld. "I had six cars last year. The one I liked most was a Mercedes. After that I had a Lincoln Continental because I thought that was very elegant."

Elvis Presley fans received word that their idol had given himself a Christmas gift of "a snazzy Cad which sports a fitted TV set, hi-fi, shoe buffer, built-in shaving equipment, a bar, refrigerator and telephone, and it even has a place for Elvis to nap," presumably after exhausting himself with the exertions of television.

Showy mansions that fail in their function of making a house a home figure prominently in all the teen-age Hollywood gossip. A few years ago, when Edward R. Murrow was still presiding over the *Person to Person* television program and Eddie Fisher was still married to Debbie Reynolds, it became painfully evident to a nationwide audience that, in response to Murrow's request to move into the living room, the two young stars were not sure where it was.

Perhaps the most widely publicized affluent-living fiasco was the Natalie Wood-Robert Wagner break-up. As are all Hollywood romances, this one was featured as the love-marriage of the ages. As a symbol of their everlasting devotion, the couple bought a $75,000 Colonial house and transformed it into a Grecian Revival—an allegorical link with the transformation which, they said, their marriage had wrought in them.

"Bob told me it would cost around $200,000 on top of the original cost, but it would be worth it," confided a gossip columnist. The teen-age lovers tore down the walls separating three bedrooms on the top floor and created one giant master bedroom with two huge bathrooms. The bedroom, in dedication to the spirit that puts affluence ahead of taste or sensitivity, was done in gold Rococco. It had an enormous bed raised three steps above a gold-tinted wall-to-wall carpet. The bed was covered with a velvet antique spread with gold fringes and topped by a canopy of the same material. Natalie's ornate six-feet-square sunken bathtub was surrounded by swans and dolphins spouting water.

It might have been symbolic, too, that the roof literally fell in on this riot of teen-age pomp. The frame of the Colonial house simply could not take it and collapsed under the strain—as did the marriage shortly afterward. But the disaster was accompanied by a bulletin to the fans that, although Natalie's gowns in the thirty-six feet-square closet were covered with falling plaster, her furs and jewels were unharmed in the built-in cold storage vault and safe. But when the marriage finally broke up, Natalie informed teen-age America: "We just couldn't face the problem of everyday living."

Except for the fantastic amounts of money involved in teen-age Hollywood's "everyday living," the fan magazines' gossip columns read much like their counterparts in high school newspapers and yearbooks all over the nation. Both imitate each other. Both have in common the standardization of goals and the publicizing of private feelings. There are understandable elements of rebellion against the conventions, but the rebellion is concerned with appearances rather than substance, with intensity rather than depth. "I respect different kinds of people," said Tuesday Weld, "as long as they have a goal, an ambition of some kind—even if it's an ambition to be a bum—if they do it thoroughly. If someone is thoroughly no good, I respect him."

It is the impact of this indiscriminate search for new symbols and new heroes that makes the destructive, amoral teen-age star of television's and filmdom's thriller-product a dangerous phenomenon, just as the indecent show of tasteless riches in the teen-age movie colony makes a worrisome model. There can be no doubt that the teen-age stars provide the models of hero worship, not for the teen-age elite but for the drifting mass of youngsters in search of a pattern of life.

Not all teen-agers, by any means, are dependent on the Hollywood hero-production machinery. Some still find, and others are beginning to find again in such new solitary pursuits as science and technical experimentation, the launching platforms for soaring aims. But for too great a number the onslaught of the mass media and of the publicity mills, grinding out phony patterns and reinforcing personal resentments, has substituted mass movement and psychology for solicitude and the personal struggle toward maturity.

9 *Books and Magazines: Misleading Memories*

There is no accurate way of measuring the percentage of the book market made up of teen-age readers. While many teen-age books are written and published annually, ranging in quality probably about as widely as do adult books, teen-agers also read much adult literature, good and bad. Adults' reading and the purchase of books is a matter of personal choice, in contrast to the music, the drama and the other forms of entertainment presented on the public airwaves and in public theaters. The teen-age tyranny, therefore, does not threaten the production of books in the same measure as it does the mass media. Nobody need complain that, because of teen-age domination, he cannot find a good book to read in the solitude of his own home.

Nor is there an accurate means of estimating the amount of reading done by teen-agers. The accounts differ greatly. Dr. Gallup's survey claims: "One third of the college and high school students and one half of the working youth said they had not read a book in the four months preceding our survey." At the same time, librarians and many high schools and most better colleges have reported a very marked revival of teen-age interest in books, partly as the result of tighter academic standards.

Among those teen-agers who had been reading books, according to the Gallup survey, high school and working youngsters listed *Exodus, Gone With the Wind* and *Hawaii* as their favorites. Fiction led by a wide margin. *The Yearling* and *Catcher in the Rye* are getting to be the new classics. In fact, one college instructor said that he no longer assigns "Catcher" to any of his classes since he knows that almost everybody has already read it.

It is fair to say that teen-age reading habits follow those of the rest of society. In homes where books are cherished and kept accessible (admittedly a minority), teen-agers grow up with the habit of reading. But as a nation, America is not to be considered very book-minded, and this, too, is reflected in teen-agers. In addition, today's teen-agers, even the most literate among them, are faced with a far greater variety of distractions than were their parents.

Even among the group of able learners, according to a report by *The P.T.A. Magazine,* "reading has a lot of competition. They [the teens] divide their time between watching television, reading, visiting with friends, automobile riding, and other activities." About half reported that they watch television more than they "read for pleasure."

As for the teen-agers' other reading, the Gallup report said that youth concentrates on newspapers, with almost 90 percent of those questioned reporting that they read at least one daily. The survey added the suspicion, however, based on youth's incomplete and shallow information on world affairs, that many of the young people (not unlike their elders) concentrate on non-news or entertainment sections. Although they claim to be turning to world affairs first, they do admit that their next move is to sports for the boys and the comics for the girls.

Dr. Gallup says that 79 per cent of the young people report they look at, or read, magazines regularly. Leading in the magazine field especially designed for teen-agers is *Seventeen,* a runner-up is *Ingenue. Seventeen* is essentially a combination fashion and service publication in the pattern of *McCall's* or *Good Housekeeping.* Presumably its readers are being readied for graduation to *Mademoiselle* or *Glamour* magazines. *Seventeen* claims a readership of girls betwen the ages of thirteen and nineteen, though the upper limit may be somewhat lower. In addition to editorial and advertising content on the latest fashions, it offers much "how to" advice on everything from haircombs to college entrance and, of course, dating. *Ingenue* follows a similar pattern on a slightly less sophisticated level.

For younger girls there is the Girl Scout publication *American Girl,* addressed to the "tween-agers" or the girl who is training to be a teen. *Calling All Girls* aims roughly at the same group, from eleven to sixteen—but getting steadily younger. This incidentally is the pattern which follows the pressure for faster and earlier "social" maturing. It is very likely that girls begin to read these magazines at ages eight and nine and graduate from *Seventeen* before they are sixteen.

Boys may turn to *Boy's Life,* the official Boy Scout publication which claims more than a million and a half readers. Their ages do not appear to be as sharply subdivided by reading habits. Articles tend to stress sports, along with more general "how to" service features. They usually feature a young hero with whom the reader can identify. Many other boys' magazines are fairly narrowly specialized, dealing with airplanes, technology, automobiles, sports, science and hobbies. There are strong indications that society concentrates on teen-age girls in pushing notions of romance and early maturing, probably in the hope that these budding matriarchs will pull their dates along with them into the split-level world of the affluent social whirl. Since the boy, if literature and screen are to be believed, is expected to grow up to be an amiable boob anyway, it is just as well to let him have his fun tinkering with his hobbies. Another factor, of course, is the biological one of the relatively slower maturing of boys in their teens.

On the more school-related side, teen-agers may subscribe to the separate levels of the *Scholastic* magazines—*Senior Scholastic* for grades ten to twelve and *Junior Scholastic* for the upper elementary school and junior high school years. Both contain special news roundups, along with articles and columns.

The same publishing enterprise provides *Practical English, Literary Cavalcade, Newstime, World Week* and *Co-Ed.* These, however, are supplementary classroom reading rather than typical teen-age fare. Similarly, on the more serious side (although not necessarily for classroom use) a private nonprofit organization called Future Homemakers of America publishes *Teen Times,* a magazine for "Future Homemakers of America" which stresses home economics but with less of the personal fashion-consciousness of *Seventeen.*

In addition, there is a literal flood of teen-pulps cluttering up the nation's newsstands. A few titles, such as *Teen Screen, Modern Teen, Teen Parade, Teen World, 16 Magazine, Hollywood Teenager, Teen Times,* and *Confidential Teen Romances,* may convey the general picture without calling for detailed description. All this is, of course, "augmented" by the "adult" movie magazines, the confession magazines, the Rock 'n' Roll magazines and the specialty publications such as the ones aimed at the hot-rod and drag-racing crowd. And, of course, most of the major monthly women's magazines have special advice columns for teens. One of these used to be authored by disc jockey Dick Clark until the controversy over payola gave him some unwanted prominence and the column quietly disappeared from the publication's table of contents.

Perhaps the most noticeable trend in many of the teen publications is the groping for sophistication. An issue of *Ingenue,* for instance, featured recipes "for a sophisticated Hallowe'en party" in which "chic rather than kids' party type food" would be served.

And, of course, there is always the problem of getting adults to "understand" the teen-agers' problem, described so eloquently by the misunderstood teen-heroine, Tuesday Weld. For the nonstar youngster, *Ingenue* featured an article that asked: "Do American Mothers Understand Their Teen-Age Daughters?" In fairness to the magazine and in contrast to Tuesday's drastic approach to mother, *Ingenue* suggested a compromise. It said:

"Our survey shows that you and mother are worlds apart but the problem is yours! Here's how you can make mother understand you and your mixed-up world." Somewhere in the article, the gap that is said to divide the two worlds is described with terrifying pungency: "Teen-agers as they exist at this moment in history," said *Ingenue,* "are a relatively new invention—so new they are baffling everyone, including the experts. . . . In a world changing so swiftly, the best-intentioned mother may actually be handicapped rather than helped by misleading memories of her own adolescence in the dark ages of only a few decades ago when life was simpler. . . ."

10 *Advice Books: Fractured Freud*

To deal with the teen-age revolution and gather profit at the same time, there is an ever-growing number of books, pamphlets, articles and columns on adolescent problems. Parents are already veteran teachers of "how to" books on every subject from sex to finger-painting. Teens themselves are fast becoming conditioned to opening a "book" instead of opening their minds when faced by a problem.

Like tranquilizers, advice books are a form of processed instant relief, not really helping to solve a problem, but making the reader "feel better fast." With few exceptions, they read as if they had been written by the same mythical author—everybody's legendary well-adjusted fairy godmother—who has a standardized explanation for every problem and is bland enough not to offend.

Books for the younger generation offer canned syndicated advice on every area of teen-life—sex, parents, money, etc.—in another dreary illustration of the creeping impersonalization of adolescent culture. Like adult books on the achievement of popularity written by famous movie and TV stars, teen-idols set forth hints for teen-happiness. Some of the chapter headings in Pat Boone's *'Twixt Twelve and Twenty* give an idea of his approach: "The Happy Home Corporation," "Your Personal Gold Mine," "God Is Real," and "Dreams Do Come True." Pat confides to his readers: "One way I found to begin to control the three 'In's'—insecurity, inconsistency, indecision—was to get my values straight. I had to ask myself questions. Why am I trying to impress people?" In his chapter on parents, the singer has one section devoted to "normal" parents and another for "extreme" parents, to cover the field.

As for kissing, Pat says it "is not a game. . . . Take it easy. Keep to the middle course. No extremes." Hints for being attractive: "Take the middle course. Stay with your age group. Don't rush. Play by the local ground rules without too much protest. That way, you won't foul out. Above all, be friendly, be kind . . . and have fun!"

"Possibly not every teen-ager needs outside help, but every parent does—if only to keep his own course straight and his perspectives clear," writes Thelma C. Purtell in *The Intelligent Parent's Guide to Teen-Agers*. Several themes run through most advice books for parents. Most important is the plea that parents must "understand" what is *really* bothering their teen-agers, not just what they *say* is bothering them. Another is the stress on the complexities of the modern world. All of it leads to a heavy dose of amateur psychiatry packaged for home use. Thus, *How to Live with Your Teen-Ager* by Dr. Dorothy Walter Baruch offers this fractured Freud:

"Junior's drive to beat the cop
Hides his wish to beat his pop."

A cartoon which shows a teen-age daughter hurling plates on the kitchen floor has mother (who has been to a psychology class that afternoon) saying:

"Talk out your hates,
Don't drop the plates."

And to underline the difference between the understanding parent and the one who has yet to see the light: mother and father are looking at an unflattering caricature of the latter, drawn by Junior. Dad (who is psychologically still unoriented) is upset at being pictured as "a fool." But mother (as usual) knows better. She has done her case study homework. "But he acts as though you were a wise man far more since he's drawn how he feels," she says.

Parents, in other words, are told to view teen-age hostility without any reaction other than sympathy and amateur psychiatry. The permissiveness of early childhood merely is pushed up one notch into adolescence. Having been pals rather than parents before, they now become a mixture of part-time providers, part-time social workers. But while adolescent hostilities do, of course, exist and should not be given exaggerated importance, the teen-ager who finds rudeness and disrespect accepted and explained away as a natural phenomenon merely revels in his victory over adult society. There are even strong indications that adolescents are testing their power at least as much as they are rebelling, and they fully expect and want to have a limit set for their actions.

There is nothing intrinsically wrong with the idea of advice books, which at least give parents the consoling feeling that they are not alone. Their problems are shared by many others. But inherent in the books is the built-in danger and illusion of American society: a naïve faith in the availability of a standard set of rules on how to solve every difficulty. The harm is in expecting too much from the pat prescription which institutionalizes the teen-ager just as every other aspect of modern life tends to be institutionalized. Already pushed toward conformity by their adolescent insecurities, nothing could hurt teen-agers more than to make of them a subdivision of humanity, thus setting them apart from mankind and delaying unnecessarily the day when they might be considered human beings rather than bundles of problems.

Psychiatrist Bruno Bettelheim suggests that modern man, rendered insecure because his physical toil is no longer essential for purposes of self-preservation, is also insecure as a parent.

"At this point," he writes, "modern youth becomes the dreaded avenging angel of his parents, since he holds the power to prove his parents' success or failure as parents; and this counts so much more now, since his parents' economic success is no longer so important in a society of abundance. Youth itself, feeling insecure because of its marginal position in a society that no longer depends on it for economic survival, is tempted to use the one power this reversal between the generations has conferred on it: to be accuser and judge of the parents' success or failure as parents." This is aggravated in a culture which expects children to go beyond the achievement of their parents, even though it does not usually turn into such brutal tragi-comedy as the patronizing gift of a Cadillac by a teen "singer" son to his "Dad."

Perhaps the best working examples of the kinds of insecurities that plague parents and teen-agers are the recordings of questions in columnist Ann Landers' book, *Since You Ask Me,* a masterpiece of its kind since it plays both sides of the field, with some chapters telling parents how to cope with their children and others reversing that order. Much of it is sound and simple advice. "Teen-agers are eager for independence but they are afraid of it, too," said Miss Landers, for example. "They want more freedom but they aren't certain they can handle it."

One letter from a teen-age girl, a true classic in its straightforward simplicity, told Miss Landers: "I have two problems—my mother and my father. They are driving me nuts. They don't realize I am a grown woman of fifteen . . . I need more freedom and I wish you would help me out by putting this letter in the paper so they can see it. And please hurry your answer. I think I'm cracking up."

A father's plaintive letter asks: "Our daughter got mad at me yesterday because I failed to take a telephone message properly. I didn't get the boy's last name. How did I know she was dating three fellows named Jack?"

Miss Landers tries not to be either too serious or too psychological—and she is honest. But the majority of advice books are little more than a further exploitation of teen-agers and their problems. They are largely entertainment, with the soothing aside to the reader's conscience that he is "doing something."

The "advice books" often degenerate into educational jargon that must make bright teen-agers squirm, if not laugh. Picture a boy or girl reading this typical piece of advice:

"If you can find within yourself patience gradually to work out with your parents your changing role, you and they will develop confidence in one another. As a result, you can, without too many fears and too much guilt, move ahead in self-development to stand at last as an individual in the world outside your home. Most parents fervently desire the mutual respect and trust resulting from this joint effort. They are eager to help you learn to develop independence from them because they know that by being willing to give you up they earn your love and friendship."

If this is slightly ludicrous, the line taken by some books is downright dangerous. Many of them continue in the "permissive" tradition that sees the home as a democratic bureaucracy of committees and equal rights (usually with the understanding that, in a conflict, Dad ought to be the one to be persuaded to give in to the more up-to-date majority).

Typical for this view is the advice contained in William C. Menninger's *How to Be a Successful Teenager,* which insists in a chapter on "How to Live with Parents," that three heads are better than two. Therefore, "one of the best ways to maintain family peace and insure co-operation is by holding family councils periodically about important matters." Expecting youngsters to obey orders from their parents, without such parliamentary procedure, is actually described as "undemocratic."

The ideal family portrayed in this book goes into conference at least once a month to "discuss various family affairs," almost always including "the budget, in which everyone has a voice." This specifically means a discussion of the amount to be spent for food, shelter, operating expenses, clothing, recreation, health, education, savings, insurance and personal allowance (with teen-agers presumably determining with an equal voice what Mother's and Dad's allowances are to be) so that "no one gets too much at the expense of others."

But, the book goes on, money is only one aspect of these family parliaments. Other issues may include "whether the family's vacation is to be spent fishing or sightseeing."

This approach puts the stamp of approval on the misconception of equal voice for all family members. This would be serious enough; for it inculcates in young people the idea that authority, based on experience and greater responsibility, counts for nothing. It is the sort of attitude that leads to the *non-sequitur* question, "It's a free country, isn't it?" as an excuse for every self-centered act. It leads to the peculiar concept that laws and regulations can be flouted unless they have first been voted on, not just by those in positions of responsibility and authority but by everybody.

But even more appalling is the image created by this pseudo democratic theory of the family itself. It is a picture of a group of strangers who, though equal in voting rights, only meet on formal occasions to thrash out specific issues, with a view toward peaceful coexistence. It introduces into family living a political concept which, in the name of harmony, destroys the special bonds of a family. These ought to be far closer, and totally different from national or international democracy. While a nation needs the formal procedures of parliamentary rule in order to fuse widely divergent interests into a harmonious and lawful organization, a family that must resort to such measures is off to an impossible start.

It is an inverted idea of democracy as well as of education to believe that the less mature ought to teach the more experienced. Social worker Irene Josselyn, in a United States Government pamphlet on *The Adolescent in Your Family*, emphatically underlines this point: "Often what they [parents] mean by independence is that he [the child] should take more initiative in doing what they wish him to do. But what they wish is rarely made clear."

What most advice books fail to mention at all is that the removal of adolescents from parental authority, adult standards, and mature criteria has created a whole new set of problems, which might have been avoidable. But they cannot be avoided by merely accepting all the present adolescent ways and teen-age actions and interests as unalterably part of modern life. Such defeatism leads, at best, to tinkering with surface symptoms; at worst, to adult adjustment to teen-age mores.

Rebellion and protest have, of course, always been important ingredients of adolescence. But like any other vital, youthful force they can be controlled, directed and civilized by a purposeful and cohesive adult society. Today's danger is that, instead of giving young people some tough and specific rules on which to cut their teeth, society is reorganizing around the demands and preferences of youth (to the accompaniment of the sideline cheers from commercial exploiters). Ironically, it is possible to provide young people with so much "understanding" of all their actions that they are robbed of the chance to rebel and test their strength, and in testing learn, grow up and mature. Turning merely to the proper chapter in an approved advice book to determine the next step is no substitute for testing and searching.

11 *Teen-Age Shopping: Water Pistol and Brassiere*

"Those V-J babies turn fifteen this year and walk into your store . . . or some store." This is the triumphant opening blare of an advertising brochure for a leading manufacture of dresses for the "modern Young Adult Woman."

No matter what other segments of American society—parents, teachers, sociologists, psychologists or policemen—may deplore the power of teen-agers, the American business community has no cause for complaint. The consumer market is steadily and constantly growing younger. At present, there are close to twenty million teen-agers in the country. By 1970, the nation's total population will be 20 per cent bigger, but the proportion of people under thirty will increase by 30 per cent.

The implications of the increase in the nation's "young" population are important in terms of the rising influence of the most eloquent and the most readily listened-to group, the teen-agers. Eugene Gilbert, President of Gilbert Youth Research, which specializes in advising business concerns on policies of marketing for the teen-age customer, estimates that as of 1960 the buying power of high school and college students directly led to the purchase of ten billion dollars' worth of merchandise a year. Within a decade there will be 25 per cent more youngsters under the age of fifteen and 40 per cent more ten-agers altogether. This is a fact of business life that cannot fail to make manufactures and sellers rub their hands with corporate glee. Nor need they wait the full ten-year span for the increasing boom; two thirds of the teen-age growth is expected to take place within five years, reflecting the flood of war and postwar babies.

Just what is the teen-age market? To define things clearly, if somewhat arbitrarily, the group under consideration is that aged twelve to twenty, primarily teens in junior and senior high school. As a reflection of adolescence itself, the wants and whims of teen-age consumers come in an infinite variety. There is the twelve-year-old girl who proudly buys her clothes in the "Tween-Teen" department, using her first lipstick and experimenting with a still often unnecessary brassiere, named "Allowance," "Little Angel" or "Freshman" in her honor. Sociologist Reuel Denney reports that the shopping list of a twelve-year-old suburban girl included "water pistol, brassiere, and permanent."

At the other end of the scale is her eighteen-year-old sister, who is likely to be approaching the altar since 50 per cent of today's brides are under twenty. She is buying all the traditional household items plus a variety of appliances which have found their way into the modern bride's hope chest. The following year, still before she leaves her official teens, she is very probably making the first of her many trips to the layette departments of the local stores.

On the male side of teen-age, the grooming for junior high school social life demands purchase of deodorants and various complicated shaving gadgets, whether functionally required or not. Interest in clothing varies with the temporary fad of the surrounding crowd. This is followed by the first car, if economically possible, at the earliest age legally sanctioned in the various states. The older brother, at eighteen, is probably beginning to wonder about the expenses involved in marriage and "starting a family."

In the business world, it has become almost a cliché that the most basic sales and promotion principle is to catch 'em young. What are the immediate resources of the young that can be caught as a prelude to more lucrative, lifelong buying habits? According to *Teen Times,* the magazine for the Future Homemakers of America, weekly spending for seventh graders ranges between 30 cents and $8.50; and for high school seniors it is between $1.65 and $19.50. More than half of the seventh and eighth graders (ages twelve and thirteen) "decided alone" how to spend their money and about the same proportion of all teen-agers from eighth grade upward used money for snacks between meals, records, hobby materials and magazines, for gifts for their friends, for school supplies and contributions to church and/or community groups. A little fewer than half of the students were found to be putting money into savings.

More revealing than these separate statistics is the cumulative purchasing power of the teen-age group, according to the same sources. During 1959, the then total of eighteen million youths spent an average of $555 each "for goods and services not including the necessities normally supplied by their families." This requires some underlining and elaboration: Quite obviously, a substantial amount of additional money is spent for what might be called luxury items beyond the necessities, paid for by the parents at the teen-agers' urging; and the $555 figure (undoubtedly higher by now) must be reinterpreted with a sober note that the "average" includes many teen-agers in the slums and lower income areas who have little or nothing to spend, making the peak annual total for substantial number of adolescents considerably more than $555. In order to put matters in some comprehensible perspective and to provide a yardstick of comparative values, the average annual pay of teachers in the lowest-income state (Mississippi) is only slightly in excess of $3,000.

It should not come as a surprise to hear one teacher, Herbert R. Coursen, Jr., a member of the English department at the Choate School, comment rather bluntly in the *Independent School Bulletin*. He quotes from a pictorial essay on "the teen-age consumer" in *Life* magazine which describes a suburban young lady of seventeen who manages to spend some $4,000 of her "reasonably well-to-do father's" income each year. Along with seven bathing suits and a personal telephone, her budget itemizes $1,500 a year for clothes, $1,300 for bedroom decorations and $550 for entertainment, not including "a jaunt to Hawaii for having survived high school."

"On summer vacation days," the *Life* story had originally reported, "she loves to wander with her mother through fashionable department stores, picking out frocks or furnishings for her room or silver and expensive crockery for the hope chest she has already started." What worries Mr. Coursen is not so much the specific "case history" nor even the comparison of a teacher's salary with this teen-ager's "budget"; it is rather *Life's* editorial note that "more and more teen-agers will be moving up into Suzie's bracket." And still worse, the article added: "Her parents' constant indulgence has not spoiled Suzie. She takes for granted all the luxuries that surround her because she has had them all her life."

If this is true, Mr. Coursen asks, the question ought to be: "To what extent are our emerging generations likely to be pre-decayed?"

Finally, the *Teen Times* economics survey revealed, again underlining the imbalance in distribution, that while one seventh-grade girl reported absolutely no personal financial means, another had $40 to spend per week.

These are the basic facts. They are, from the business point of view, promising enough for one enterprising firm in California to build a shopping center for teen-agers only. It cost $2,500,000, has six shops, a studio, an ice-skating rink, a bank "for small accounts," a swimming pool and a milk bar.

How did the teen-age economic scene come to be what it is today? The key, of course, is the general prosperity of the country and the unprecedented affluence of many families. If there is more to spend, more will be spent. But the special mushrooming of teen-age purchasing power has its roots in the more basic sociological developments and values of modern society.

The permissive philosophy of child-rearing and the rushing of adolescent social development had opened the floodgates of material generosity. Once it becomes desirable for twelve-year-olds to go to dances, the question of "what to wear" also becomes a major one. In a society which judges prestige very largely by outward appearance, what an adolescent owns automatically turns into a yardstick of the entire family's place in the sun. If mothers are interested in their daughters' early dating, they will tend to close an eye to, or even encourage, the purchase of luxury items and services, from nail polish to permanents.

One of the most obvious signs of the times is the newest status symbol of the affluent teen-ager: a weekly trip to the hairdresser. Young girls begin regular visits as early as twelve and thirteen. Many start going before a "big" event while they are still in grade school. And not just for a haircut.

Teens are now veteran salon-goers. The increase in business at a spot these young ladies regularly visit is welcomed by the owners. Parents pay the bill and Cleopatras, Junior Grade, wallow in their newest luxury. A sophisticated Manhattanite of fourteen said: "I started coming about a year ago because this is one of the things teen-agers do."

The tidal wave of teen tastes sweeps over the objections of schools, parents and even the more sensible hairdressers. The teens know what they want—and they get it. One vocational, high school department head said: "They not only come in wearing these highly teased styles; they do them here, and laugh in our faces when we tell them that they are not good styles." As usual, mothers wring their hands and go along.

Perhaps the last word on teen appearances at beauty shops was the remark of one manager who said he could not tell how many teen-age girls were customers because "they all look so old."

The pressures mount. Teen-age society, with its own status symbols, forces adult society to lend a helping hand and pocket book—or lose face, both with the teen-agers and with the adult neighbors who are also parents of teen-agers. A comically descriptive example is the experience of a foreign diplomat stationed in New York. His young son, who attended the local high school in a suburban residential neighborhood, had long and unsuccessfully tried to persuade his father of the need for a television set. One day, the boy's parents learned that their son had been making the rounds of his American neighbors and telling them that his father was "acting un-American." The pressure of his newly acquired peers had had its effect.

There are other complicating factors. The parents of today's teen-agers grew up during the Depression. They have known hardships and uncertainties, topped by World War II. Their children are not only part of another generation; they live in a different world. Although they hear a good deal of talk about nuclear war, they have no concept of the real meaning of war. They have (since we are not talking here about the underprivileged teen-agers of the slums) no knowledge of the meaning of real want and poverty, of the possibility of not being able to make or command a living. They have not been conditioned, either by their education or by their experiences, to make the achievement of material possessions dependent on hard work. Their picture of the American way of life is complete with home, car, family, children and all modern conveniences as a matter of birthright, without postponement for financial reasons. And if they cannot afford these American privileges on their own, then presumably the family stands ready to help them along. If they are concerned with poverty at all, it is like studying a baffling foreign concept. The needy in the slums are an object of compassionate interest, but they are divorced from the "normal" teen-ager's personal life and experience. There is rarely the feeling, which briefly visited even the children of the well-to-do during the Depression, that there, but for the grace of God, go we.

All this has fundamentally affected the thinking and behavior of the parents as well. Although they cannot help wondering during occasional nostalgic reminiscing sessions whether their own lives and characters have not been made richer as a result of the hurdles they had to clear, they would be unnatural parents if they wanted to subject their children to similar hardships. They cannot re-create conditions of the past. Affluence like poverty is a wave that engulfs. It would take a superhuman effort to keep its comforting waters from sweeping the young of today along with them.

This does not mean that all are equally well off; but as long as material wealth is a mark of distinction, parents are understandably reluctant to explain to teen-agers that the neighbors, because they are wealthier, can give their children more money, luxury and economic freedom. As a natural consequence of materialistic values, this would be tantamount to an admission of failure.

This is a point at which reforms, if any are to be made, are most essential and at the same time most feasible. But it requires strength of character for parents to swim against the stream, especially in the tyrannical environment of status-conscious and superficially homogeneous suburban living. The obvious example is that of many European societies where middle-class parents traditionally have not been ashamed to teach their children that economic differences need not be hidden from view, like skeletons in the closet. Children can be encouraged to better themselves. But parents must not fear being despised by their children for lagging economically behind their neighbors.

To change such values is a slow and laborious process, not without painful unpleasantness at first. Eventually it could and should lead to a broader judgment of human achievement than along a sliding dollar scale. European university professors, for instance, command considerable respect, even though they are not very high on the economic scale. This ought not to be misread as a justification of low academic salaries in the United States, but it ought to mean that the contemporary argument that higher pay for teachers is the only road to respect and recognition merely reinforces the wrong scale of values.

This requires an early new look at these values—in school. Somewhere along the road the all-important concept of equal opportunity has become confused with a claim to equal possessions in an affluent society. The right to the free pursuit of happiness has been misinterpreted to imply the right to insist that economic comfort be delivered to each and all on a silver platter. More that that, in a school which frowns on intellectual competition, which holds that comparisons and the recognition of differences are harmful to children's emotional growth, the atmosphere is protective. It then becomes a natural chain reaction for youngsters who have been sheltered from recognition of differences to grow into teen-agers who have developed the habit of expecting to own what the rest of the crowd owns. Thus, teen-age society is aided in extending its tyranny over adult society.

This is particularly true in homes where the status-seeking insecurity of parents is heightened by the sense of the inferior position of being relative newcomers on the American scene—first- or second-generation immigrants or, more recently, the newest of new arrivals in a new suburban community. Unsure of their own place in the world, they are even more intent on buying a place for their children.

In terms of the teen-ager's impact on the economy, the fact is that the pace-setters of our current adolescent society know only prosperity and security and expect only more of it.

Looking at the adolescent's changing role in the economy, Dr. Bruno Bettelheim points out that in the America of the past, and in less affluent societies today, the older generations depended on youth for economic survival. This was to adolescents a source of strength and self-respect. But what is the situation today? "In many respects youth has suddenly turned from being the older generation's greatest economic asset into its greatest economic liability," Dr. Bettelheim writes. "Witness the expense of rearing and educating youth for some twenty or more years, with no economic return to be expected."

What the psychiatrist deplores, business and industry welcome. Confirming the Bettleheim thesis but turning it into a theme for rejoicing, Eugene Gilbert writes in his book, *Advertising and Marketing to Young People*: "Just look at youth! No established pattern. No backlog of items. No inventory of treasured, and to many adults' way of thinking, irreplaceable objects. Youth . . . is the greatest growing force in the community. His physical needs alone constitute a continuing and growing requirement of food, clothes, entertainment, etc. It has definitely been established that because he is open-minded and desires to learn, he is often the first to accept new and forward-looking products."

The adolescent, in addition to being a spender on his own account, is a Pied Piper who sets the styles and the trends for adult society to follow. He becomes not only the future buyer whom the merchants wanted to catch young for his own sake; he is also the child that shall lead his elders to new forms of spending. Adolescents are now the pioneers of conspicuous consumption.

Leaders in industries which cater to the distaff side are now regularly making speeches in praise of their new young pacesetters. The teen-ager and the young woman in her twenties are hailed as the two most important consumers of cosmetics. And teens of both sexes spend more than three hundred million dollars on toiletries. The fifteen to nineteen group is reported to have spent twenty million on lipstick, twenty-five million on deodorants and nine million dollars on home permanents in a typical year.

Among the clothes which have graduated from high school and college to high fashion are the raccoon coat, hip-hugging pants, knee-length skirts and bandanas. Not long ago, a manufacturer of women's slacks, the biggest "young" fashion of all, told reporters: "The biggest market is among high school and college girls and young married women. [Many are still in their teens.] Once these girls become accustomed to slacks they continue to wear them. That's why more and more older women are wearing them."

An important manufacturer of "Young Adult Women's" clothes, Bobby Brooks, Inc., proudly states in the annual report for 1961: "As in each year of our history net sales exceeded those of the preceding year. The annual increase has been 18½ per cent over the past ten years." (There was no recession here!)

Bobby Brooks considers her Young Adult a wealthy shopper who "expects in a week as much excitement as would have lasted her mother a month in 1940." In addition: "Driving home from school with a boy had reached date-status earlier, but now add driving to school in the mornings. So she's on inspection around the clock. Means more clothes. More girls than ever before are going to college, where they insist on wearing the 'best campus' styles, but want several copies."

For those who might be misguided enough to think the case has been overstated, Eugene Gilbert reported that the teen-age girl (fourteen to seventeen only) spent a grand total of $773,776,000 in 1960 on her "back-to-school" clothes and other necessities. She will please her public at all costs. No wonder stores have redesigned their departments to please their younger shoppers. They would be foolish indeed to ignore a demand like this. The older customers find their way back to the less desirable locations to spend their money.

Eugene Gilbert adds that "fashion enters the teen-age girl's life at about fourteen years of age, and approximately two years later she is buying nearly all her own clothes." Actually, however, some kindergarten teachers in the suburbs complain that some of their charges have, in recent years, begun to compare not only their styles but the prices which their mothers paid for them. Fashion leaders like Dior and Lily Daché are now designing clothes for girls as young as six.

But teen-age has long ceased to be a satisfactory category for the complicated fashion market. The field has been scientifically broken down into levels, a reflection of today's habit of organizational tidiness.

First, there are the sub-teens. Their age ranges from ten to thirteen, another indication of the tendency to move the social clock ahead as fast as possible. Generally, a sub-teen is in junior high school, or just below, and considers herself quite grown up, compared with her "girl years," roughly seven to ten.

From age thirteen to fifteen, girls have graduated into full-fledged teenhood, as far as fashions are concerned. According to Mr. Gilbert, they tend to shop alone and are interested in "sophisticated styles," similar to the "juniors," the upper division of teendom. Unhappily, the teen usually suffers from the indeniable, but not unalterable, fact that her figure has not yet achieved "the real junior look."

The junior, according to the fashion trade, is a girl whose figure has completely matured and, according to Mr. Gilbert, "many girls in this age group [sixteen and up] may already be engaged or even married."

It is an interesting phenomenon that although American society tends to be so shy about the comparison of intellectual achievements, the comparison of what has come to be known as the "vital statistics" is considered sufficiently crucial to have been neatly tabulated by the Commodity Standard Division of the United States Department of Commerce. What emerges is the following government-approved schedule in inches:

	Bust	*Waist*	*Hips*
Sub-Teen (size 12)	31½	25½	34
Teen (size 14)	33½	26½	36½
Junior (size 13)	35	26	37

Out of it all we get a neat mixture of salesmanship, physiological fact and the kind of educational jargon that makes everything from the school lunch to the teaching of the alphabet subject to psychoanalysis. Thus we learn from the marketing experts that "the retailers who are successful in selling to these groups of girls are those who have recognized their emotional and physical needs." The high-priced fashion consultant Tobe & Associates, for instance, suggests that stores develop special departments for teens and sub-teens and that this kind of specialization should include lingerie and accessories, the latter being a particularly important tool for the development of impulse buying. Note that no opportunity for the "educational advancement" of adolescents is to be left to chance!

A Midwestern department store examined the motivation of the "sweet sub-teen" and found that she is not only fashion conscious but wants to be grown-up. She needs clothes, not primarily because she is outgrowing what she owns but because "this is the age when her social interests begin to enlarge. She doesn't feel herself a child, is ready in some instances to start dating, and if she doesn't date, is attending more parties . . ." She begins to feel the "need" for accessories, and (so the experts conclude) an "accessory bar" suited to her tastes and needs will often prove to be a "prime traffic spot" in the department.

Since these marketing studies find that, while this subteen group is already largely permitted to select its own clothes but is still sufficiently unsure of its tastes and desires to need adult help, the sales force must be ready to provide such assistance. But as the aim is to sell, these masters at adult guidance are urged to avoid the authoritarian attitude that might be expected from a teacher or an old-fashioned parent. Instead, their counsel as well as the counter display ought to consider "the whims and fads" of the adolescents themselves. In other words, in salesmanship as in so many other approaches to the teen-agers, the part played by adults is not to try to guide youngsters, however diplomatically, toward adult tastes and standards but rather to reinforce the standards of the adolescent culture. Then the result is given the stamp of adult approval. Since teen-age fads are known to be of short duration, the retailer is warned to keep stocks low and be ready to respond to new fads and depend on rapid turnover.

Interestingly, the youngsters themselves, even though they follow the commercially reinforced fads, are smart enough to be conscious of the fact that fads are silly and not quite respectable. Thus, when *This Week* fashion editor Joan Rattner asked girls at colleges around the country what they were wearing, each school self-righteously protested that its campus was definitely not "faddy." But when the spotlight was turned on reality, the truth was what manufacturers knew all along and responded to: Bermuda shorts, dirty sneakers, trench coats, circle pins, long sweaters and T-shirts were practically the uniform of the moment.

The final irony is that adults, instead of trying to influence teen-agers, are so caught up in the cult of youth that they gradually adopt teen-fashions for themselves. The older sister comes first, and soon mother follows. Many fashion experts trace the rise of sportswear and "casual' cloths directly to the influence of "Teen Queens." Nor is this confined to the girls. Bruce Gimble, President of Gimble Brothers Department Stores, says: "Men, taking a cue from the boys, now want slimmer pants, trimmer suits, sharp colors, some hot shades and gaucho shirts—all of which started in the boys' business. ... If the trend to sports shirts and blue jeans is not checked, our future generation of fathers may well be dressing in exactly this fashion when they go to their jobs as executives and white-collar workers." This may merely buttress the "palship theory" of parenthood, If, as many theorists try to make us believe, the ideal father-son relationship is to be one of pal-to-pal (not even man-to-man) rather than adolescent-to-mature adult, than it follows that those who act alike, think alike and talk alike should also dress alike.

Perhaps the best indication of the respect in which the business world holds the adolescent dollar is shown in the rise of teen-age charge accounts. If credit is extended to so many less influential and less affluent segments of the population, surely teens should be able to say "charge it" just like their elders.

A recent newspaper advertisement, offering "teen-age charge accounts," emphatically made the point that no adult signatures were required. "Pick it out. Take it with you," the ad told its young readers.

A closer look at the growth of teen-age credit and charge accounts is essential to an understanding of the controls exercised by the adolescent society over adults. A recent survey by *Seventeen* magazine showed that teen-age charge accounts have doubled since 1959 and that some of them start with thirteen-year-old shoppers.

What are these charge plans, alternatingly known as junior, student, youth or "honor" accounts, or glamourized by some enterprising stores with such prestige labels as "Starlet Charge Account," "Campus Deb Account" or "14 to 21 Club?" How are they different from the traditional, informal habit of small-town stores to extend credit to the children of their good customers, as a favor to the parents?

While details may differ, most of the teen-age accounts have top limits of between $25 and $50, although occasional stores raise the ceiling as high as $100. Some retailers offer youngsters straight installment credit which calls for a new contract with each item purchased. One California jeweler advertises "Going Steady Ring" at $12.95, for "nothing down, payments of 50 cents a week."

The question of parental approval is a subtle and, one suspects, purposely vague and confusing one. Although the teen-ager usually opens the account himself (answering certain credit questions about his allowance and/or part-time jobs), most stores require parental okay, either by phone or in writing. Almost none, however, ask parents to vouch for the accounts. In some cases, the retailer actually tells the parents that they will not be held legally responsible.

Few, if any, shops ever try to take parents to court in order to make good on their offsprings' bad debts. The legal questions involved would be complicated and tedious. Even more important, it would be damaging to the store's teen-age public relations to sue over relatively minor sums. The good will of young shoppers is worth more than occasional small losses. In many cases, a letter or phone call to the parents is generally enough to do the trick. Parents naturally want to protect their own good name and that of their children. So, it is not surprising that the National Retail Merchants Association reports the teen-age record of paying up is good. In fact, stores have claimed that, either in spite or because of legal restrictions on minors' responsibilities for debt, holders of junior charge accounts have proved to be better credit risks than their elders.

Advocates of the extension of teen-age credit point to this good payment record as an argument for the "educational" value of teen-age accounts. They compare it to the junior savings bank accounts which are part of many public school programs to encourage thrift and, in the progressive tradition, even to help as an incentive toward arithmetic. Retailers like to claim that their teen-age accounts are an effective way to educate youngsters in "money management" and help them develop self-reliance. One West Coast store, summing up such fine educational sentiments, said: "The establishment of accounts for this potential market will not only produce lucrative results for stores, but will also serve the community by developing responsible credit risks through proper guidance of these young people."

A. L. Trotta, Head of the Credit Management Division of the American Retail Merchants Association, says: "If a store was primarily interested in additional sales, this could be best accomplished by having teen-agers use their parents' accounts, where thay would be spending more freely than where they had to charge purchases to their own accounts."

Critics of teen-age credit take a dim view of these arguments. They suspect, first of all, that here is just one more example of society making a virtue of an unpleasant fact of life, in order not to come to grips with it. Credit, like cancer in the comedian's parody of cigarette advertising, is considered to be "good for you." There is, of course, no denying that, as the proponents of teen-age charge accounts stress, we live "in a credit society." Thus one must not only learn to live with it, but extend it. Progress, in the view of those who try to make society's faults look virtuous, is the surrender to the inevitable.

They would not therefore look the facts squarely in the eye, as television critic Harriet Van Horne did in a review of David Brinkley's NBC program on the "re-possess agent" —the man who takes away the dishwasher, the sofa or the car that has not been paid for. For a quarter of a n.illion families, Miss Van Horne reported, "the threat of repossession is a recurring nightmare."

The victims of "credit society" in this instance were two

nice young people, Mary and Dick, with an income of $110 a week and an indebtedness of nearly $20,000. This is how Miss Van Horne described the scene:

"Discussing her unpaid bills with Brinkley, Mary blamed the charge-plate system and 'the nice Welcome Wagon lady' who arranged for additional charge accounts even though Mary and Dick were poor credit risks. Dick, who works at motel, said he had no regrets about spending $500 on children's toys because 'we can at least keep the kids' world secure.'" (A pathetic confirmation of the progressive disease of making youngsters 'secure' through excessive material possessions.)

Earl B. Schwulst, President of the Bowery Savings Bank of New York, testifying before a Senate subcommittee on a bill concerning consumer credit labeling, attacked teen-age charge accounts for teaching habits of spending instead of thrift. He called it, perhaps with excessively dramatic emphasis, "something like teaching the young to use narcotics." Even if the comparison is strong, it is at least fair to ask whether everything that teaches the established ways of society must be considered educational, without questioning to what extent those ways are worth teaching.

In his book, *Buy Now, Pay Later,* Hillel Black reported that in some places teen-agers could be charged interest of 33 to 80 per cent on their charge accounts and that neither the parents nor the children realized that "such exorbitant charges are being made." If the educational argument is carried forward to cover even this extreme case, the defenders of teen-age credit would probably insist that being fleeced is an experience which can teach young people a valuable lesson. If we "learn by doing," why not also learn by being had?

Returning to Dr. Denney's report of the twelve-year-old girl who had "water pistol, brassiere and permanent" on her shopping list, we find the sociologist's suggestion that this aging adolescent was demonstrating not only the tremors of physiological transition but also the elements of precocious purchasing power. "If you can buy as an adult, you *are* an adult," writes Dr. Denney. "And one of the main things about adult buying in the United States is that you do not need ready money to do it. 'Grow up now and pay later' might have been the motto of the youth who quickly spent a fantasy four thousand on a credit-card spree. . . . With the exception of the children of some three million families in the United States that survive on a brutally low income, there are few young men who cannot scrape up enough to buy a second-hand car."

In spite of the proponents of charging-it-for-teens, for educational or commercial reasons, the future of the teen-account is not completely clear. Senate investigations have provided a slight brake to their mushroom growth. If such criticism can make merchants slow down the trend, it is fair to suggest that they are not quite completely convinced that credit extension to teen-agers is really a healthy development.

Perhaps the real problem is best put in perspective, not by learned opinion and self-seeking surveys, but by comic-cartoon heroine Penny, the perpetual teen-ager, explaining the whole matter:

"No," says Penny, "I can't see you tonight, Bunny. Father and I are going to go over my budget to see why I always go over my budget. . . . The Federal government is running at a deficit, the state and city are running at a deficit, heavens, I'd feel positively disloyal if I didn't have a deficit! . . . I notice Father lectures me most about my money handling when *he*'s overdrawn at the bank. I think teen-agers should co-operate budgetwise, it makes fathers happy and doesn't interfere much with spending. Well, things will be pretty organized around here till father's last bank statement wears off and he gets his credit card accounts paid up!"

Perhaps one of the hardest adjustments for the old-fashioned proponents of the prerogatives of an adult society is the acceptance of the "bride market" in the fashion economy as part of the teen-market. The fact, however, is that in 1960 at least half of all brides were teen-agers. And for a full comprehension of the self-perpetuation of teen-age values and tastes, it must be added that over half of the married teen-age "women" have one or more children. Eugene Gilbert advises all those interested in the bride market to keep in mind four essential points:

1. The new peak age of marriage for women is eighteen.
2. The median age of marriage for women is just above twenty.
3. One third of all "first children" in the United States are born to mothers aged twenty years or less.
4. The American marriage age is now lower than that of

any "peasant country" in Europe.

To the market researchers these statistics can have only one implication: they "not only make it imperative to regard the bride market as the one logically following graduation from high school or college, but also the market destined to grow and keep pace with the rising birthrates of the 1940's." Even the most forward-looking experts on adolescent purchasing habits have a hard time keeping up with the times. Norman Lobsenz, writing in *Good Housekeeping* magazine, tells of "a recent semester at a Southern high school" during which fifty-two girl students announced they were going to be married at the end of the term. He also put on the record the story of a junior in a Midwestern high school who "married, fathered a baby, and got divorced all in one year." The bride market, in an increasing number of cases, does not just follow high school graduation but parallels the high school curriculum.

At any rate, the market researcher observes accurately that "the fever of getting married young has risen to such a pitch that girls who are not engaged before they finish college feel that they stand a good chance of becoming old maids"—and the merchandising watchdog adds ominously: "They may be right."

Seventeen magazine made a "Hope Chest Study" and found that girls as young as thirteen and fourteen are interested in collecting household items for future homemaking. Nobody thinks it odd to find silver and china tableware advertisements aimed at teen-agers. "You get the license. I'll get the Lenox," the famous Lenox China slogan, now is more likely to address itself to teen-age boys and girls than to young adults.

If there is still some of the aura of novelty around the idea of the marrying teen-ager as a major segment of the nation's apparel and housewares market, few parents of any era will consider it news that teen-agers eat. The hungry, growing boy or girl raiding the icebox has been one of the oldest stand-by situations of family comedies, from comic strips to television.

It is hardly surprising then that organized sellers have latched on to this market, especially since many teen-agers, rendered mobile by the family car or their own, do much of the family food shopping. Even when they don't, their food preferences influence the family menu. That this is not necessarily a promising manner of guiding the nation's eating habits may be guessed from a report by the United States Public Health Service that 52 per cent of the teen-agers' diets are poor and that the teen-age girl of this affluent society tends to be "undernourished." She may, at the same time, be overweight.

Some food chains have made special efforts to attract young customers. Food Fair stores even offer scholarships to encourage promising youngsters to study this aspect of food retailing. Others sponsor social activities and picnics. One large chain lets teen-agers run its stores for a day each spring.

The boom in snack foods is evidence that the after-school snack has become as much of an American institution as the coffee break. But there is no longer any need to go home for this ritual; the local luncheonette offers anything from a cheeseburger to an "Awful-Awful," the updated and bigger version of the old banana split, which appears to have derived its title from the description, "It's awful big; it's awful good!" Some eateries which cater to the teen trade have an "honor roll" for hearty souls who have eaten three in order to get a fourth as a free dividend.

More often than not, the late evening raid on the icebox has been replaced or augmented by "TV snacks" throughout the evening. Here, too, teen-agers have been the pacesetters, and their parents are increasingly falling in with the trend. We would like to discount reports of teen-age girls living for weeks on chocolate peppermints and stuffed olives or on cold boiled potatoes spread with grape jelly and salted peanuts—not because we don't believe it possible but because, if true, there is always the danger that adult society will feel a compulsion to prove its youthfulness and join in.

Naturally, what the "right people" eat is of great consequence. Elvis Presley, for instance, according to a communiqué from his press agent, has described his favorite snack as a sandwich consisting of mashed bananas and peanut butter on white bread.

As might be expected, the teen-age influence on the record market is nothing short of fantastic. When John Molleson reported in the *New York Herald Tribune* that Van Cliburn, the pianist, has sold one million copies of his recording of Tchaikovsky's Piano Concerto No. 1, he added that this work "thus becomes the first classical album to top the million mark in the history of the recording industry." Such teen-age idols as Elvis Presley and Johnny Mathis have had no trouble attaining similar sales records.

According to trade sources, there is no way to measure the direct impact of teen-agers on the record market with a specific percentage figure. There is agreement only that the influence is great and out of proportion to the actual dollars spent by the kids themselves. The record industry divides its market into two groups. First, there are the sub-teens (ages nine to fourteen). They account for 20 to 25 per cent of the total industry dollars. This is the market for the fan clubs and the sales of single records. (A "single" in the trade is a 45 rpm. record, seven inches in diameter, with one tune on each side, which usually lists for 98 cents.) Here, also, is the huge juke box and radio disc jockey sale. Manufacturers can count on forty-five million singles for juke box sales.

The point to remember about this market is that it is dominated by air time. In order to sell "singles" a record must be aired—and frequently. This is where the influence of the teens on programing is most evident. The audience of disc jockey shows and juke boxes is the "sub-teen" crowd. Its preferences are listened to by everyone, willing or not.

The industry knows that in this group the girls buy three quarters of the records and are more "loyal" fans than boys. The organization of the fan clubs, therefore, favors male singers.

The remainder of the market is composed of fourteen-year-olds and up and is called the "adult" market. This is the "album" market. (Most albums are 33⅓ rpm. discs, twelve inches in diameter, with six tunes on each side. For a "pop" the usual list price is $3.98; for a "stereo," $4.98.) *Billboard* magazine points out two reasons why the album-buyers are growing younger: First, they have more money and are getting hold of more all the time. Second, as the family gets more affluent and can purchase stereo, the youngsters inherit the monophonic equipment. Consequently, the tide of Rock 'n' Roll albums is swelling all the time.

Adults who find it difficult to accept or adjust to teen taste in music can find some small and short comfort in some juke boxes which have introduced a recording-length interlude of silence, purchasable at the regular nickel price that most frequently sets off Rock 'n' Roll and other teen-age art forms. For the most part, however, adults are a captive audience.

In sheer economic terms, teen-age music is big business with a vengeance. Paul Anka, one of the 1962 wiggling headliners, could command $25,000 in one appearance at Atlantic City. Elvis Presley's earnings have been reported in excess of two million dollars a year. Presley souvenirs—hats and shirts, blue jeans, teddy bears, pencils, pads, and pins—were reported to have chalked up three million dollars in sales during the years the teen-idol was in the army. In less than six years, the singer is reported to have sold seventy-five million records and he has several gold records for each time he topped the million mark.

According to the fan magazines, Presley gets about thirty-thousand fan letters a month and the manager of his enterprise is said to send out a million and a half Christmas cards to admirers to keep the market alive and profitable. It would be foolhardy indeed to underestimate the commercial value of Presley's statement that he bought a Rolls-Royce because he "learned to love good engines" when he was a truck driver.

Apparently unaffected by past TV investigations, Dick Clark is estimated to be making $500,000 a year. Another popular disc jockey of the teen-age crowd is reportedly working for his Ph.D. in sociology and making $500,000 a year "on the side" for his time on the air. Teen-age millionaire singer, Bobby Darin, is reported to be active in real estate.

Most of the teen-age singing idols have skillfully combined their "art" with extensive business enterprises. Paul Anka, who also writes "music" has a business office in mid-Manhattan for his Paul Anka Productions, the Spanka Music Corporation, and Flanka Music Corporation, all of them affording him a reported annual income of over one million dollars a year. His record "Diana," which bemoans the fact that an "older" young lady of that name fails to return his undying love, has sold more than nine million discs here and abroad.

Lest anyone think it too easy to become a business tycoon by becoming, managing or supporting a teen-age singer, he should look at another set of the record business figures. Since the advent of Rock 'n' Roll in 1954 (the R 'n' R "pop smash" was "Rock Around the Clock" by Bill Haley and

The Comets in 1954), new record companies have appeared on the market at the rate of about three a week. This explosion in record companies means that *Billboard* has eight thousand label names on file, of which about six hundred to eight hundred are active during any one year, and few survive. Many may be tax dodges formed by a "singer," his manager and possibly his brother-in-law. The stakes are high, but the going is rough in this most fickle of all markets.

These reports from the teen-age market are, of course, only the parts of the iceberg that are visible above the water's surface. The two vital questions, and the second more important than the first, are: how does all this affect the economy and how does it affect teen-age life and culture?

David Riesman says in *The Lonely Crowd:* "The boys' weeklies [of the past] and their American counterparts were involved in training the young for the frontiers of production [including warfare], and as an incident of that training the embryo athlete might eschew smoke and drink. The comparable media today train the young for the frontiers of consumption—to tell the difference between Pepsi-Cola and Coca-Cola, as later between Old Golds and Chesterfields."

Among the headaches of parents of modern teen-agers is the continuous tugging on the family purse strings—not for the essentials but for extras and luxuries. Financial columnist Sylvia Porter writes that "the family with one or two or more teen-agers to feed, clothe, educate, entertain must switch its spending patterns and cut down on many purchases the adults may want—unless the family's income is in a sharp upswing. That father and mother may not consider what they are doing as a significant influence on the markets for housing, furniture, appliances, etc. . . . but when they are multiplied by millions, the influence is unquestionable." Miss Porter concludes that teen-agers "are compelling increasing numbers of families to spend comparatively less of their incomes on the goods which dominated shopping lists in the 1950's. It'll be the mid-1960's before these teen-agers begin marrying each other and again changing the age characteristics of our population. As of these early 1960's the teen-age torrent is a fact of economic life which demands a lot more attention than it is getting."

This insufficiently observed revolution is one of dramatic contrasts. In the old days of an agrarian economy, children were an economic boon to the family. The more children there were, the more "hands" in the field or behind the store counter. Today, the greater the number of children, the lower must be the standard of living for the parents. The crisis comes in the early teens when girls must have dresses on a par with those of "the other girls," and the boys want their cars—in addition to the increasingly costly bills for education. At the same time, there is increased pressure to keep the young out of the labor market as long as possible. In fact, the opportunities for part-time work have dramatically decreased. It is ever more difficult for the unskilled, the semi-skilled or the part-time worker to find jobs. Since economic security depends on an ever rising level of *completed* education, teen-agers remain unemployed boarders, with expensive tastes and prominent voices in the family's spending habits.

This is how Riesman puts it: "One must listen to quite young children discussing television models, automobile styling, or the merits of various streamliners to see how gifted they are as consumers long before they have a decisive say themselves—though their influence in family councils must not be underestimated. Children join in this exchange of verdicts even if their parents cannot afford the gadgets under discussion; indeed, the economy would slow down if only those were trained as consumers who at any given moment had the wherewithal."

The "trade" knows this, even if parents do not. Women's service magazines have columns devoted to the teens, usually inspiring them to become consumers of fashionable products. Even in the free send-away columns of one of the major women's magazines, three out of ten items on an average are for the teen-agers—"How to Be a Better Teen-Age Driver," by an insurance company, "Party Cooking for Teens," by a soup manufacturer or "Bowling Fun—Ten Pin Tips for Teen-Agers," including the hints on the proper attire for the young crowd.

A newspaper in Washington has found it profitable to have a special Teen-Ad section, with the advertising concentrating on records and dance bands for hire at teen-age parties. Such commercial teen-age entertainment is available, an ad says, at reasonable rates for fraternities, teen clubs, dances and other similar occasions.

"Today the future occupation of all moppets is to be skilled consumers," says Riesman.

The inherent dangers ought to be self-evident. The skillful promoter within the economy is in his heyday if he can impose teen-age standards and criteria on the adult market, with taste and quality taking a back seat. As for the teen-agers, they become at once the victims of the promoters and an at least partly unwitting pressure group on adult society. But perhaps most serious for themselves, they are given the power and the need to age before their time.

12 *Wooing the Passion for Possession*

The advertiser's business is to sell. His job is to look for markets, preferably easy markets, potential buyers who can be persuaded without much effort. If, in addition, these customers-elect promise to do a little missionary work of their own to set off a buyers' chain reaction, then they are the advertiser's dream. Increasingly, in recent years, the American teen-agers have been the advertiser's dream-come-true.

It is part of the American tradition that the children educate their parents in the new culture. This is the way of life in a young and growing civilization and in many ways it's a good and encouraging phenomenon. In big cities, parents often were immigrants, anxious to become part of America. Children learned the new language easily, adopted new customs and ideas and helped their parents speed their more difficult adjustment. Thus the traditional way of most other cultures was reversed: instead of the parents' role of handing the traditions, customs and taboos down to their children, American children were encouraged to help parents break with their traditions. Teen-agers thus became the authorities on "the way things are done here." It must be remembered that, in contrast to the class-divided and caste-molded older countries, the American ideal of an open society with universal educational opportunities inevitably gave many children more schooling than their parents had enjoyed. High school was no longer reserved largely for children of high school-educated parents. College was no longer the privilege of the college-educated upper middle class or the children of professional people. Beginning with the pioneers and continuing through waves of new arrivals right up to the latest influx from Puerto Rico, children moved ahead of their parents.

Essentially, this concept of the open society is the basis of the American success story and the justification of the American revolution. The hidden danger is that as a result of the stress on the new and the intensity of the effort to break with the past in order to rush into the future, the parental position is undermined (if not actually and purposely sold out) and the adolescent power exaggerated beyond the bounds of good sense and decency.

Salesmen of all sorts know this and exploit it. Within recent years they have turned this knowledge into a highly developed science. The direct advertising pitch geared to and blared at the teen-age market, after careful conditioning of the pre-adolescent age groups down to the nursery school tots, has become a vital subdivision of the advertising industry.

Let's look at the campaign to win the young dollar from its pre-kindergarten beginning. Children still in their play pens watch television, the electronic baby sitter. A toddler is told via the home screen to ask for a special cereal, and mother buys it. After all, it probably is as good as any other brand, and so—why not make Junior happy? One survey showed that 94 per cent of the mothers interviewed said that their children had asked them to buy goods they had seen on television. We can only assume that the children of the other 6 per cent were as yet too young to talk. The pattern, once established, becomes increasingly more difficult to break. It works up to a habit almost as compelling as drug addiction by the time the youngsters reach teen-age.

Reading experts find that pre-school children, who are not yet able to read, often have no trouble recognizing the word "detergent."

Eugene Gilbert says: "An advertiser who touches a responsive chord in youth can generally count on the parent to finally succumb to purchasing the product. . . . Parents generally have little resistance or protection against youth's bombardments. Thus it becomes evident that the youth market is the one to reach. We, of course, do not mean to picture the parent as the downtrodden object at the mercy of his offspring; but it is not to be denied that a parent subjected to requests from the youngster who thinks he is in dire need of an item, witnessed on television, may find it easier to 'give in' rather than dispute rationally with a highly emotionalized child. This is not to say that we advocate merciless hammering by the advertiser through the child to make papa purchase thousands of unnecessary objects, but we do mean to reiterate again that the young person's influence is not to be underestimated."

Keep in mind that Gilbert is writing for the advertisers. The tepid defense of the parents' limited rights might be called advocacy of the soft rather than the hard infant-sell. Or, to put it another way, the commercial exploiter of children is asked to avoid killing the Mother Goose that can be counted on to lay unlimited golden eggs.

If there is any doubt about the dangers of the exploitation of children, a recent review in the *New York Times* about the return of a delightful children's show, *Kukla and Ollie,* ought to be the tipoff. "The advertising, which it was Fran Allison's unenviable lot to deliver yesterday," said the otherwise enthusiastic critique, "is anything but attractive. Children were told repeatedly to ask their mothers to buy a particular brand of pretty mutliple vitamin pills. The use of a child as a club to force adult purchase of a product is a tiresome practice at best. But when applied to the subject of any kind of pills it is something that should be scrupulously avoided. Do-it-yourself medication does not belong in a children's hour."

This is merely the preparation for the appeal to the teenage and truly lucrative market. Since social maturing is being rushed, the categories of customers become increasingly younger, a fact not overlooked by the advertiser. The magazine of the Girl Scouts, *American Girl,* explained for instance: "Being a teen-ager is a goal in itself, something to be reached. In the jet-tempered '60's we think you hear 'teen' considerations earlier, and we have coined these new age names for you—tenteen, eleventeen, twelveteen." From there, the discussion moves on to those "who have already achieved thirteen" and "use their first lipstick, wear their first nylons and first bra sooner than girls ten years ago."

Now, move from the editorial content to the advertising messages in the same magazine. A bra ad explains: "Whether you're ten or a teen, you are moving into the delicious, delightful stage known as womanhood. . . . Teen-form understands every girl's secret wish." There is one bra called "Littlest Angel—the bra that expands as a girl develops." The inevitable question is whether the manufacturer is not the mother of "every girl's secret wish."

Whether the motives are entirely commercial or semi-psycological (in line with the educational stress on rapid social development), the effects are beyond question, and they have been ably and aptly summarized in the birthday editorial of the seventeenth anniversary of *Seventeen* magazine. The reminiscing editorial said:

"When *Seventeen* was born in 1944, we made one birthday wish: that this magazine would give stature to the teenage years, give teen-agers a sense of identity, of purpose, of belonging. In what kind of world did we make our wish? A world in which teen-agers were the forgotten, the ignored generation. In stores, teens shopped for clothes in adults' or children's departments, settling [they had no choice] for fashions too old or too young. . . . They suffered the hundred pains and uncertainties of adolescence in silence. . . . In 1961, as we blow out the candles on our seventeenth birthday cake, the accent everywhere is on youth. The needs, the wants, even the whims of teen-agers are catered to by almost every major industry. But what is more important, teens themselves have found a sense of direction in a very difficult world. . . . Around the entire world, they are exerting powerful moral and political pressures. When a girl celebrates her thirteenth birthday today, she knows who she is. She's a teenager—and proud of it." Even allowing for poetic license in the description of the "forgotten" teen-ager of 1944, there is no question at all that influence of the adolescent group over the adult world has skyrocketed in the intervening years.

But the clincher followed in a "birthday ad" for the same issue, headlined "SEVENTEEN IS 17 . . . Isn't everybody?"

"Of course we know that everybody can't be 17," the ad said. "But *Seventeen* magazine lives in such a whirl of a girl (girl thirteen to twenty) that sometimes it seems as if every body who is anybody must be 17 or thereabouts. Because teenagers are the most powerful, influential, affluential chunk of the population today. 'Twasn't always thus. . . ."

"It is easier to start a trend than to stop it," and some trends turn into runaway tides.

The Telephone Company offers eloquent testimony of the power of the teen-market. In telephone booths, the advertising slogan proclaims that "the teen-ager thinks the Princess is super. She says the colors are really dreamy. And she's doing extra chores so she can have her own Princess extension."

Another advertisement elaborates on this theme: "Your teen-age princess will appreciate the privacy of her own Princess extension—and you'll appreciate the resulting peace and quiet around the other telephones in the house!" (In other words, if you can't lick them, buy for them!)

And in order to make sure that the message won't get lost among the group, the ad (which first ran in the adult press) was revised for *Teen* magazine to invite the underprivileged, still forgotten, in the ranks: "Come over and see my new Princess phone—Dad and Mother gave me one for my birthday. It's right here in my room. Daddy says he got tired of my talking while he was trying to read or watch TV."

That not everybody takes as enthusiastic a view of this development as the Telephone Company was hinted at in a report from Washington by Martin Tolchin in the *New York Times*. Interviewing Mortimer Caplin, Commissioner of Internal Revenue, who had just moved his family to the suburbs of Washington, Mr. Tolchin writes: "The Caplins are startled by some of the social habits of Washington's younger set. They were surprised to discover, for example, that many teen-agers had their own telephones and their own listings in the telephone directory."

In fact, Mrs. Caplin said bluntly: "I think it's barbaric. Teen-agers have sort of taken over the world. Families should learn to share things—beginning with the telephone."

Mrs. Caplin might be even more shocked to learn of the direct approach by a large typewriter manufacturer to insufficiently co-operative parents. "How to convince your parents you need a new ——— Portable by ———," advises the ad. "Just fill out and mail us this coupon and we'll write to your parents. We'll tell them you're interested in the ——— portable and explain that it can help you to get better grades. You can tell 'em how much more fun homework becomes after you get your ——— portable ..."

While the typical teen-age beauty ads promising fast relief for skin blemishes still speak prominently to the adolescent market, the glamour product, once confined to the adult population, now appeals to the teen-age girl and her boy friend. One of the most sophisticated French perfumes pictures a boy and a girl, sitting in the classroom after the rest of the gang have gone home for their snack. "When he seems to solve all your problems . . . you're ready for ———," the ad says. And one of the equally sophisticated (and expensive) competing perfumers advises: "Is it all right to wear ———in the classroom? Yes, if you don't mind being the teacher's pet." One of the American glamour beauticians has a special complexion package at a lower "back-to-school price."

And since teen-age begins in infancy now, there is, of course, a special appeal for the slightly less affluent younger market—the reading-readiness training of the beauty field. Along with the ads for the expensive scents, there are special offers of "Perfumes for Pennies—Just twenty-five pennies, to be exact, bring you any of the purse-size fragrances . . ." Each of the four are advertised with a stuffed animal in a wooded setting.

There is a column called "Dressing Table Talk," a quickie course in beauty culture, on how to rate an A for appearance all through the school day, and the vital warning that "gym class can ruffle a hairdo, so arrive prepared with comb, brush and hair spray, a jiffy trick to perform between classes . . ." Another between-class trick is performed by a make-up remover which is offered in quantities of "from ounces for teens, to gallons for teams."

Such slogans as "Kiss of Perfection" and "Go steady with ———" tell their own story. Girls are initiated into the "glamour trap," as it was described on a National Broadcasting Company commentary, earlier and earlier. A teenage girl told the television panel that she was going to the beauty parlor because "Mama told her that was the only way to get a rich husband."

An idyllic picture of two teen-agers, with the girl literally "carried away" in the boy's arms on a pillared veranda with a castle in the distance, is the background of an ad for an expensive brand of china tableware. Not to be outdone, a manufacturer of sterling silverware advertises: "The second most important choice you make . . . Whether or not you've chosen *him,* now can be the precious moment you select your sterling . . . Use your heart—and your head." Like other advertisers, this one offers a free booklet, "My Hope Chest Diary." Those who have not kept pace with the precocious bride "market" may be surprised, but (as pointed out earlier) hope chest items are now firmly part of the teen-age magazines. It is not at all unusual to find hints for "Foods Boys Love" and booklets on "How to Plan Your Wedding" as part of the same teen-age literature.

If this seems like rushing things, what about the life insurance company which asks fourteen-year-old boys to think about retirement insurance? There are those who consider this—and almost any practice of making youngsters old before their time—an educational rather than a commercial enterprise.

Another question is the propriety of the use of schools for advertising purposes. In New York City, with the official sanction of the Board of Education, schools hold "dress up days." If this were merely an attempt to get youngsters to understand the importance of dressing neatly and with care, there could be no objections. But last year, the "day" in cluded the modeling of boys' and girls' clothes furnished by two of New York's most fashionable stores and identified as such. The practice of commercial fashion shows in public schools would be questionable by any criterion; but in this instance, the high school was one which enrolls a large number of children from the poorest sections of the city. To parade in front of their eyes the kind of material goods which are far beyond the reach of most of the audience is not only commercial exploitation of youth; it is downright cruel.

Yet, the fact that schools are being "used" quite regularly emerges clearly from Eugene Gilbert's chapter on Institutional Advertising to Young People."

"Among the pitfalls an advertiser must avoid is the intrusion of more advertising material than is acceptable to the school board," Gilbert warns. He asks the advertiser to be aware "that if his material is accepted, it may still not perform the job of building up a future market." The answer? "The indirect approach" and what might be called the camouflaged sell. "If the educational material is such that the youthful viewer or reader cannot buy or influence his parents to buy the particular product, then the advertising expenditure for the production of such material can only be regarded as an altruistic gesture," Gilbert counsels.

Perhaps it is an indication of the stamina of that old guard which believes that the exploitation of pupils for commerical ends is not one of the schools' legitimate missions that Gilbert adds the observation: "Another important but unfortunately unavoidable practice that cuts down the advertising value of educational material is the practice of teachers cutting out or removing the name of the sponsor. The teacher may cut out the name in written literature, may stop the projector before it reaches the end of the film where the name of the sponsor is mentioned, or may work with but one copy of the material, using it for demonstration purposes only, and the student will never see or know the advertiser's name."

That this hazard is not too severe, however, was shown by a survey which found that four out of every five students polled had received some kinds of commercial material in school and that much of the commercial message was remembered by them. Gilbert adds the significant note: "Since apparently more money is expended each year by business organizations on educational materials than is spent on all the textbooks per year in schools, the use of such materials has become perforce an accepted medium for reaching the youth market."

Fortunately for the advertisers, the minds of many educators are as flexible as those of advertising account executives. Phrases about the importance of linking the classroom and real life come easy and tend to justify anything.

Not all authorities take so broadminded a view of the growing exploitation of teen-agers. *The P.T.A. Magazine,* official publication of the National Congress of Parents and Teachers, reviewed the National Broadcasting Corporation's weekly commentary on world events, called *Update.* The program is specifically aimed at the high school group, and the review called it "excellent" in its "lucid, lively exposition," supported by maps, pictures and other visual aids.

The critique added: "This admirable program has one bad blemish, however. The sponsor intrudes four disruptive, incongruous commercials for cosmetics into every thirty-minute presentation. Aimed directly at adolescents, the advertising seductively links lipstick and complexion aids with popularity. This crassly commercial diversion of young people's attention from cosmic events to cosmetics and dating is distasteful and deplorable."

In a recent program, what was presented as a regular "feature" and therefore thinly disguised as part of the program itself turned out to be a running plug for the book *Tiffany's Table Manners for Teen-agers.* But this simple commercial message apparently was not enough. A well-turned-out teen-age couple, of high school age, was shown romantically dining at one of Manhattan's more fashionable and expensive restaurants. Nor were they merely *shown* dining there; the commercial for the restaurant was plainly part of the commentary. Clearly, from the advertiser's point of view and expectation, the high school and junior high school crowd (the specific audience of *Update*) had come a long way from the hamburger-and-Coke kind of date and the corner drugstore romance.

And so, not unlike inflation, the teen-age purchasing spiral moves upward. "While parents often blame their teen-agers for their extravagance, most of them have no conception of the pressures that are being put on your people to buy and keep buying," warned Thelma C. Purtell in the *New York Herald Tribune*'s magazine, *Today's Living*. She quotes a Madison Avenue expert as saying: "This is a market rich enough to turn any marketing man's head."

The issue is summed up with stark honesty by Bernice Fitz-Gibbon, advertising and merchandising consultant for *Seventeen* magazine, as quoted in the magazine, *New York State Education*. Miss Fitz-Gibbon told a "fashion clinic" which discussed back-to-school ideas:

"Your fashion department is the wooing chamber. Get the teen-age fly to come into your parlor and little by little the web will be spun. Then when the girl marries you haven't lost a customer. You've gained a gold mine."

Miss Fitz-Gibbon referred to the teen-age girl as "a woman with means" who has "a passion for possession." She urged retailers to go after "the teen tycoons, not in the sweet by-and-by, but in the much sweeter now-and-now."

There is, of course, nothing intrinsically wrong with the advertising expert's desire to create or exploit a market. That is her business. But it should not follow that parents or educators need either agree with this purpose or play into its hands. The question that must be faced by those who are responsible for the future of today's adolescents is how to assure that teen-agers grow up with more satisfying drives than "a passion for possession."

The only bright spot on this gloomy horizon of the victimizing of youth is the good sense of at least a small and hopefully growing segment among the teen-agers themselves. Miss Purtell reports: "Despite the tremendous advertising pressure on young people to spend, the happiest note yet may be that the young people themselves will put an end to their exploitation. After all, they're children of the age, and the blandishments have been flickering before their eyes from birth. They can get tired of them, or may not be as gullible as some people hope."

Indeed, there are small signs of some unrest. An editorial

in the school newspaper, written by the elementary school youngsters of Plandome Road School in Manhasset, New York, said this: "The advertisers try to get people to buy their products. At Christmas time they make their commercials look so realistic and wonderful that children believe that what they see on television is real. . . . 'Go, get Smoochy if you want a little kiss! Press her arms like this, you get a little kiss.' I'm sure you've heard this at least five times. Who in the world needs a doll that kisses?"

Who, indeed? Maybe the children are growing tired of adults who want to rush them into growing up and spending money. Perhaps some of these youngsters are about ready to tell them to peddle their wares elsewhere and let children and adolescents be young again.

Maybe . . . But it's too long a gamble. Youth has a right to some protection, and not only against dope peddlers. Child labor has been declared illegal for good reasons. The exploitation of children's spending power for commercial reasons is no less obnoxious than the exploitation of the children's physical resources. Both threaten their normal growth and development. Each, in its own way, hurts society—teenage and adult.

13 *Goals: Indigestion Through Affluence*

"Gee, Officer Krupke!
We're very upset,
We never had the love
That every child oughta get.
We ain't no delinquents,
We're misunderstood.
Deep down inside us, there is good.

Officer Krupke,
You're really a square.
This boy don't need a judge,
He needs a analyst's care.
It's just his neurosis
That oughta be curbed:
He's psychologic'ly disturbed."*

These excerpts from a song in *West Side Story* were put into the mouths of delinquents from the slums. Admittedly, slum delinquency is not the issue and the problem here discussed. But the teen-age tendency toward psychological self-diagnosis and self-pity is as pronounced among the "normal" teen-agers in the affluent sector of society as among the under-privileged—and less justified.

Sociologists' slogans have become a new brand of patent medicine to explain away teen-age attitudes and youth's misdirected energies. This, too, is nothing new. The "lost generation" of an earlier era conveniently turned to the disillusionment over the failure of the "war to end wars." The difference here, as in practically all areas of teen-age prob-

*Lyrics by Stephen Sandheim (Columbia Records)

lems, is again that the self-analysis has begun at so much younger an age. Instead of representing the rebellion of young adulthood, it now symbolizes the self-pity of adolescence.

The convenient excuses can be stretched to cover any situation. When a critical report on the sexual excesses of high school and college students during spring vacation sprees in Florida talked about boys and girls parading naked on a hotel roof and engaging in public sexual activity, a student columnist in *The Columbia Owl,* a publication of the Columbia University School of General Studies, took a dim view—of the criticism. What, he asked, is wrong with "sand, sex and suds?" His answer, in a purposeful *nonsequitur,* was:

"Let's face it, man, the world stinks. It's not *our* world; it's not the world we would have made, but we're the ones who are stuck with it. . . . We are all responding to the realities of the Big Bomb, the Cold War, Algeria, the South, Berlin and the Wall, China, Korea, and South Africa, Auschwitz and Budapest, Franco's Spain and Castro's Cuba. Blowing off tension in a panty raid or tearing up Fort Lauderdale makes it all bearable. We're stuck with the world, and adults are stuck with us."

The scorn for the follies and failures, the bigotry and bungling of the older generation and its predecessors is well deserved. If out of the scorn are born new generations of Angry Young Men, this is not only understandable but may even be encouraging. Honest anger is not at all bad medicine. But if anger over The Bomb leads to nothing more than riots on the beach, then there is little justification for the grandiloquent alibis. Whereas Angry Young Men might set out to establish new beachheads of reform, the Frustrated Young Boys are satisfied with beach parties and temper tantrums. If teen-agers say that the adults "are stuck" with them, they are cutting off their noses to spite their faces: in the end, the new generation is stuck with itself.

And what are teen-agers in danger of being stuck with? The most sobering approach to an answer is a look at the extremes of their aimlessness, not to make them appear typical but to underline the symptoms of hidden dangers.

We repeat that we are not concerned with the vast and complex problems of juvenile delinquency. What must be faced, however, is the rise of a different kind of delinquency among teen-agers from comfortable middle-class homes. It is a delinquency that has been especially troublesome in the commuter suburbs, the semirural communities to which urban families "fled," presumably in order to permit their children to grow up in wholesome, uncrowded surroundings. Even there, our interest is not in delinquency itself but in the light it sheds on the troubles and problems, the goals and attitudes of adolescents.

A recent Senate document has said, "National and state police officials report that there are increasing occurrences of vandalism, muggings, burglaries, larcenies and crowd disturbances emanating from the ranks of those who have no reason for committing these crimes except for so-called thrills."

This is not a purely American phenomenon. A UNESCO bulletin reports that during the Christmas season of 1956 the streets of Stockholm were repeatedly invaded by thousands of teen-agers who smashed everything in sight. "There was no organization, no rallying call, no program behind it all—the mobs formed spontaneously," the report said.

Columnist John Crosby wrote: "The abundance of automobiles in the hands of the young in prosperous Sweden has brought about the Raggare, which might best be translated as hot-rodder, although the word implies a liking for girls as well as cars. . . . At night, the Raggare cruise up and down the Kungsgatan, the closest thing in Stockholm to Times Square, picking up thirteen- and fourteen-year-old girls. Off they roar to the country or somebody's apartment for blatant drinking and sex parties. . . . Some of them [the Raggare] have come from Sweden's best families."

Parallels with this kind of delinquency of the affluent may be found in London, in The Hague, in Vienna and Sydney, and in Paris as well as in Germany. Nor has Russia escaped from this problem. *New York Times* correspondent Harrison E. Salisbury reports on this new teen-age set of "hooligans" and adds that many of them are "well educated, cultured young people, sons and daughters of high party and government officials." When one youngster in Russia defined his goals, "Well, nobody wants a heart attack. What do I want? Drink . . . restaurants . . . jazz . . . money . . . women . . . a Volga [Soviet brand automobile] . . . a country cottage," a Soviet official of the older generation shrugged: "I cannot understand our young people. . . . They are growing up without ideals. They have lost their ideals."

Perhaps one problem shared by all nations in the modern world is the speed of change and the instability which follows in its wake. There has always been a gap between generations, and understanding between father and son is naturally a delicate and difficult thing. But the gap has widened enormously. The world has been changing at an ever faster pace that makes the experiences of each generation grow further apart from those of the previous ones. Parents today are bringing up children to live in a world that is not only changing violently in terms of technology and science; it is a world of comfort and security that makes the stories of privation and struggle, so real and vivid in the older generation's mind, about as meaningful as Greek mythology. It is, in toto, a *nouveau riche* world, and the basic characteristic of the newly rich is to want more and to attach extraordinary importance not only to material possessions but to the status-giving competition of out-owning one's neighbor.

If the Puritans put excessive stress on austerity, the Atomic Age moderns similarly overdo the emphasis on measurable, demonstrable affluence. The mink-lined beer-can opener is less a joke than satire. Combined with the earlier background of permissiveness in child-rearing and the submission to competitive group pressures, this cult of affluence cannot help but lead to teen-age trouble.

It is aggravated by the new American mobility. Approximately thirty-five million Americans change their homes annually—many of them by moving to different communities. Almost anywhere the "native" is a rarity, and a resident of ten years' standing is an old-timer. Large companies pick up their executives and their families like office furniture and ship them and their households across the country. The technique has been perfected to the point where professional movers are able to transplant an entire household, with hardly so much as a loss of a routine heartbeat of daily living.

But if the transition appears smooth and without a loss, there has been an intangible loss of a different nature. The stabilizing permanence of community mores—stabilizing despite their often stodgy and even oppressive pressures—has been thrown off balance. When there are so many "new people" in a town, the question, "What will the neighbors think?" tends to be replaced by "What can the neighbors see?" Visible, purchasable "things" become of prime importance.

Since shortage of space—the only increasing poverty among even the affluent—has brought people closer and closer together, in suburban developments as well as city apartments, the togetherness of modern group-living presses toward conformity without cohesion.

Since mobility tends to follow functional lines of professional or promotional requirements, families are more readily broken into compartments, with less overlapping of generations. There are suburban developments today which consist almost entirely of young and growing families, separated from the grandparents, the aunts and uncles and the other links with the past. And as the parents are often unsure of themselves and insecure in their social status (especially if they are part of the early marriage wave), the dominating force is neither past nor present. It is the future—the children. While it is sound and worthy to look to children as the hope of the future and to start them on their road, it is exceedingly dangerous to let the inexperience of the young dominate the standards of the mature.

These are among the reasons why, in extreme cases, teenagers of the modern era of affluence (rather than of The Bomb) turn to an almost incomprehensible variety of delinquency. In addition, as Dr. Kenneth Cameron of the Royal Bethlehem Hospital in London explained the problem with disarming simplicity: "It fails to be recognized that the well-fed young male, particularly with money in his pocket, has always been antagonistic to social conformity."

Specific cases of middle-class teen-age delinquency vary, but there runs through all of them a pattern of startling similarity. In a pleasant and quiet residential area of Queens, the semisuburban outskirts of New York City, seventeen teenagers were seized after they had taken $100,000 worth of loot in the course of five years of burglaries. During the hearings, the youngsters attempted to blame the community, a comfortably prosperous one, for offering too little by way of "excitement." None of them needed the money.

Several teen-agers who were not personally involved in the burglaries complained about similar lack of entertainment. Typical comments were:

"You have nothing to do. You feel like banging your head against the wall. So what do you do? You go to Utopia [a neighborhood luncheonette where the teen-agers appeared to meet and plan their 'activities']."

"This place is dead—a dead neighborhood."

"There should be a place where guys could go to take out their excess energy; instead of this, there's nothing to do tonight."

Interestingly, when trouble over teen-age parties erupted in wealthy Scarsdale (as pointed out earlier), here was the same complaint, and the same search for an answer by way of a recreation center.

But is this the answer? In a well-to-do New Jersey suburb a group of youngsters were arrested in a similar burglary-for-kicks case. The police investigators learned that the "thrill" crimes had been planned in the Leonia Town Recreation Center. While a few of the boys said they needed the money, most of them admitted that they had taken part "just for kicks and because it was thrilling." In fact, reports indicated that the group had been brought together by its joint interest in sports. All of the youngsters were members of their high school football and basketball teams. Thus, lack of an outlet for their excess energies could hardly be blamed.

In another incident, a young boy knocked down and kicked a woman on a street in Brooklyn. He made off with her purse containing $1.27. An investigation showed that he had an ample weekly allowance and $500 in bonds which he did not want to cash. His father was an advertising executive.

Among the most tragic escapades "for kicks" have been recurring narcotics parties in the best of the suburban areas. In Westchester, 251 youngsters from prosperous families were found to have been involved. Reports said that "a teen-age fad of smoking marijuana cigarettes and cocaine, heroin and opium derivatives in pills, by inhalation and hypodermic injection was disclosed."

The youngsters were found to have attended narcotics parties and had then felt obligated to reciprocate with similar parties, mostly in substantial private homes. Some of the children involved were as young as thirteen. Teen-age friends had been invited from well-to-do communities from Port Chester to Pelham. They were frequently joined by "guests" from Fairfield County, Connecticut and New York City.

Until they were presented with irrefutable evidence, the parents angrily denied the charges. But finally when one of the boys confessed, his father, with equal lack of understanding, shouted: "I should take you by the throat and kill you. I have given you everything. Where have I failed?"

One experienced educator offers the simple reply that this father and other parents like him have failed exactly because they have given their children everything. Miss Sophie Jaffe, a sixth-grade teacher in New Britain, Connecticut, told the American Federation of Teachers: "Children must learn as children that one cannot have everything one wants." She told of four-year-olds in kindergarten who boast that they "know how to get what they want."

Among the most appalling examples of teen-age delinquency, without explicable or excusable reason, was a story which exploded into the headlines of the San Francisco press during the summer of 1961. A group of middle-class boys were arrested after they had systematically and ruthlessly persecuted an elderly Jewish couple for fourteen months. One of the teen-agers was the son of a prominent officer of the city's Fire Department. Two were sons of police officers. Another was the son of a taxi fleet executive. Among them was a college student of psychology and a high school student with an A record in his academic work.

No deep grudge was involved. None of the boys appeared even to have any ideological involvement with anti-Semitism, political or otherwise. It all had begun, they explained, as "a joke." Some of the boys, sitting around at a party, decided that it would be fun to make some anonymous telephone calls. Apparently one of the boys suggested the Jewish couple as a good target because the elderly man had complained when the youngster kept riding a noisy motorcycle around the neighborhood at night.

The calls soon became a nightly source of kicks. "New boys" joined the group, boosting the number of calls—often to fifteen a night.

The calls—threatening and obscene—were only the beginning. In the months that followed, homemade gun-powder was poured over the couple's car outside their home, and the car went up in flames. At other times, the tires were slashed, paint was dumped over the car and the pathway to the couple's home, and finally a bullet was fired into one of the windows. Extending the "practical joke," an endless parade of cab drivers, deliveries of Chinese dinners and pizzas, ambulances, television repair men and, finally, a hearse, were dispatched to the home of the innocent and helpless victims until they were so terrified that they barricaded their doors and were afraid to go out.

After an incomprehensibly long period of apparently ineffective police work, the boys were apprehended. The first one to be questioned gave the stock alibi: "We had nothing better to do." Another boy, described in one of the newspaper reports as "clean-cut," said: "It's not that we had anything against Jews. It was just something to do—there wasn't much else to do." Still another explained that the game of harassment had become "the thing to do" and added that "if I had known I was hurting them by the phone calls, I never would have done it."

One of the more articulate teen-agers said: "That fellow [the persecuted victim] should have hung up the phone when we called. Instead he'd just stand there and listen." Thus, the blame begins to be shifted. It is only a short step, then, to self-pity, and the step was taken by "a good-looking curly-haired boy" who said that while the couple had "only" suffered for fourteen months, why was nobody feeling sorry for those who had gotten themselves in trouble for so innocent a prank. "What about me?" the boy complained. "My whole life is ruined." Later he added: "I tried a couple of times to get the guys to knock it off. But we kept getting new guys and they weren't satisfied. So we went along with the Gang. Then, too —we kept it up because of the Eichmann trial. We thought that worked beautifully as a gag."

After this frightening exhibition of insensitivity, he came to the clincher: "We're all pretty upset. Our jobs, education, everything is up in smoke. I've had a year of engineering . . . I planned to enroll in psychology this fall. Now I don't know what I'll do. My whole life has been burned up."

And yet, the boys were not too upset to demonstrate their interest in publicity—that other great mass-disease of modern society. One of the group asked a photographer if he wanted a smile. Another inquired of a television cameraman: "Are we going to be coast-to-coast?"

As for the parents' reaction, they at first denied that their children could possibly have been involved. When the evidence was in, one father's explanation was fairly typical of the majority's feelings: "My boys don't smoke or drink. They apparently made some phone calls in recent weeks. They thought it was a gag."

This is par for parental reaction reported by police officials in such vacation states as New Jersey, Maryland, Florida and California. They appear to agree that the most typical reception they get from parents informed by phone at night that their teen-age children have been arrested for drunken and disorderly behavior is a mixture of disbelief and anger—at the police. A routine response, say these officials, is a smug statement that "my child does not drink" and that he or she undoubtedly has nothing worse than an upset stomach. More often than not, testified one experienced police officer, the conversation winds up with the parents giving the caller a tongue-lashing for casting aspersions on their youngster's virtue. Yet the problem has become so widespread—often involving thirteen- and fourteen-year-olds—that the police on Catalina Island charge $2.50 an hour for "baby-sitting" to cover the time a drunken teen-ager is in the "care" of the authorities until the parents appear to take him or her home.

It should be underlined again that these examples of serious delinquency among affluent adolescents are cited not as typical but as extreme symptoms of a disease that, in its more routine manifestations, is much harder to diagnose and therefore more difficult to cure. It is much easier, for instance, to shrug off the outdoor sport of stealing automobile emblems. In fact, there is the story about one boy's doting uncle who bought the youngster a Volkswagen seal when he heard that his "club" required the theft of the emblem for admission. Then it merely decorated his drawer. In another instance, a passerby who berated a group of youngsters engaged in stealing a seal from a parked car was angrily told to mind his own business. "What do you care?" one boy said. "It's not your car."

How easy the transition from seal-stealing to car thefts can be is illustrated by shocked summer residents in some of the most fashionable suburbs. They report that sports cars are stolen daily from commuter railroad stations, used for the day and simply left somewhere along the road after they have served their temporary purpose of relieving the day's boredom. (It should be kept in mind that the areas plagued by this nuisance are not city slums where under-privileged teen-agers have every right to feel that there is nothing wholesome for them to do and no legitimate opportunity for them to give their youthful energies a workout. These are the suburbs which abound in beaches, swimming pools, tennis courts, bowling alleys, etc. They are the places, too, where parents, at the drop of a hint, are ready to chauffeur their children to any center of amusement and activity.)

Teen-age values are inevitably determined by the adult values around them. To students of contemporary society, therefore, it may not come as a surprise that teen-agers, according to the Gallup survey, take a permissive view of cheating, television scandals and other indications of moral laxity. The survey found that 70 per cent of the youngsters questioned across the nation believed that "most people" would accept bribes, if they were offered, on television programs. Almost half of the boys and 20 per cent of the girls said they themselves would do likewise. A high school boy said: "Payola is simply compensation for services rendered."

After the scandal involving the Columbia University instructor, Charles Van Doren, seven eighths of the students on his own campus interpreted their concept of loyalty by either sympathizing or offering excuses. In fairness to the youngsters, it should be added that sociologists studying their reactions to the scandals found teen-agers more sophisticated than their elders, making it easier for them to shrug off the seriousness of the problem. Many of the teen-agers expressed surprise that anybody could think of the quiz programs as anything but a rigged circus. Their elder's gullibility, fed for profit-reasons by the mass media of television and press alike, had understandably made them cynical.

The problem lies in the impossibility of drawing and maintaining a line between such "legitimate fraud" and the real article. The Gallup survey reports (and educators have known this to be true for a long time) that cheating on examinations, particularly in high school, is widespread. Seventy-five out of a hundred of all youngsters queried said that they knew this to be true. One high school senior explained: "Everybody tells you that you're hurting yourself when you cheat in school, but you don't really know that's true. You don't really feel that it's dishonest. Everyone cheats every chance he gets. The trouble is that kids are lazy and the competition is so great."

It is the competition for admission to "prestige" colleges and the parents' pressure toward it that is understandably given by many children as the reason for cheating. A senior class officer said: "The only thing some parents are interested in is marks. We know that we have to get the marks to get into college. How we get them doesn't matter."

New York Times reporter Martin Tolchin made a survey of student attitudes in the New York area and found that cheating occurs at all levels of academic ability and performance. Some students even tried to achieve success by doctoring their report cards, admitting the most convenient means of doing so is the practice of drawing a line through the "minus" after a grade, thus turning it into a "plus."

The president of one senior class said: "If you don't know the answer and you don't cheat, you've given up. If a person cheats, he hasn't given up." His sentiments were echoed by a girl about to enter a "prestige" women's college: "A person cheats because he wants to do better on a test. Some people don't care enough to cheat."

When asked what is wrong about cheating, few of them felt any conflict with basic principles. The closest they came to any judgment of values was that it "violated the standards of society." A class valedictorian went even further, saying that he did not see any real discrepancy between cheating and the present standards of society. "Most people who cheat don't feel that they've done anything wrong," he said.

It is obvious to anyone who follows the news that society continues to keep acceptable standards extremely "flexible." The image of success is more important than the means of achieving it. The answer to teen-age cheating is not that this has always been a practice, as, of course, it has. There is a vast difference between the age-old human tendency to try to get away with violation of rules and the permissive removal of such rules and standards in the first place. The fact that laws are broken with great regularity, far from being an argument against the making of laws, is instead the most convincing reason why laws are necessary. The "liberal" view that it is better to relax standards than to invite hypocrisy in the nonobservance of them overlooks the need of human beings for a frame of moral reference.

This is particularly true of teen-agers. No matter how strict the rules, they will always test the limits to which they can go in circumventing them. The theory that by relaxing the rules youngsters will become more honest is a sentimental pipe dream. It merely deprives them of the security of knowing right from wrong and makes it more difficult for them to decide how to behave and what to do or not do.

Expressing the opinion of his generation (which is an extension of the views of his elders), a senior at Midwood High School in Brooklyn commented on scandals in the New York school system's construction department. "The school scandals didn't shock me," he said. "You have to figure there's going to be graft in city government—that people are going to take their cut." This is merely a genteel version of a cartoon that showed two dead-end kids reading the headlines about the school scandal. "Gee," said one of them, "and I always thought them school board guys were squares."

This should not come as a shock. Teen-agers have eyes and ears. They see and hear how "the system" works. Scandals and whitewash of scandals could hardly be news to them —any more than they were news to generations before them. Perhaps the only significant difference today is that the individual is more completely awed by the complexity of the system. There is the team, the corporation, the association. Promotions come in waves like officers' commissions in armies. And so, when something goes wrong within the system there is always the fear that if the corrupt are punished, whole echelons of the "team" will suffer, too.

A boy, quoted in the Gallup survey, tried to come to grips with the issue: "You know, there are no individuals any more. There are no more Lindberghs flying the ocean alone, or real men with real names and real identities exploring the frozen North. It's all done by team work and helicopters and submarines, backstopped by a thousand scientists and technicians. Even the astronauts are not people, they're a team." It might be added (and the boy's comment came before the event) that John Glenn made a valiant effort to counteract that theory: after the team helped to put him into space, a defective mechanism suddenly required of him a demonstration of the continued importance of personal initiative, under the loneliest conditions ever devised by man. His later expression of hope that future space fights would be entirely man-operated was a much-needed sign of the revolt of the individual against corporate management. How essential that assertion of man over mass really is was shown when, shortly after the flight, a teen-ager said that he thought there should always be two astronauts in every space capsule to keep each other company and compare their reactions.

Youth is caught in the pull of conflicting currents. Adults blame teen-agers for lack of drive and idealism; yet, when opportunities for service, such as the Peace Corps, come along, many parents find such service admirable in theory (or for other people's children) but a roadblock to quick and secure economic advancement for their own sons and daughters. Even those youngsters who really want to serve are understandably alienated by the widespread feeling that the Corps is a device to create an image. Mary Anne Guitar, writing about "The Cautious Crusaders" in *Mademoiselle* magazine, quotes one student: "If I have to go out and be a good kid and give America a good image, I'm not interested. I never heard Albert Schweitzer say he was representing any particular country." (It might be added that Dr. Schweitzer's continued hold on the romantic imagination of youth is probably as much the result of his resolve to do things as an individual as of the actual good accomplished by him.)

A girl who had spent the summer in West Africa as a member of Operation-Crossroads said: "It felt good to be doing something constructive.... It also meant a great deal to me to be able to get through the whole summer, to be able to live in such a different environment. We learned to rely on ourselves so much more than we do at home."

David Riesman has commented on the same problem in the *Atlantic Monthly:* "It is exciting to watch a group of them examining in detail what American students might contribute to secondary education in Nigeria and what qualities of judgment, self-reliance, pertinacity and technique such students would need to be of real help. I have seen students who seemed, even in their own eyes, cool customers, ready to ride the organizational escalator, discover a chance to serve in an underdeveloped country."

But these are the exceptional few. The dilemma of the mass of students is captured by Philip Rieff, a sociologist, when he writes in *Harper's*: "The fact is that no one compels the young today. Therefore they must compel each other, like children left without their parents. What passes for politics among them may be more accurately described, perhaps, as their mood of excitement at discovering that they are alone and without direction from the adult world of power and responsibilities."

Wherever they turn, young people receive little strength from the adult world on which to rely. We are not here concerned with questions of religion, nor are we competent to deal with them. But there is every indication that the much talked about "revival" of teen-agers' interest in religion is misleading and exaggerated. In an effort to "capture" young people as "churchgoers," the various denominations have frequently adopted the same methods used by the schools to increase their "holding power." Like the schools, they stress the pleasant, nonessential and social aspects. There is nothing wrong with a church dance or bingo get-together; but it bears little relation to religion. Perhaps a road sign put up by a local church in California, asking people to worship because "it's profitable," is an exaggerated expression of this trend. But at least one prominent Protestant university chaplain, when asked about the depth of the religious revival, merely laughed and said: "A lot of people consider it a religious revival when they say, 'God, I need a new Cadillac.' "

In general, teen-agers merely reflect the confusion of their elders. There is no question that they are frequently more active in church activities and that there are among them those who are genuinely dedicated to religious efforts and beliefs. But many young people remain understandably cynical of religion as long as they see it turned on and off like a water faucet by too many adults. One articulate girl said: "It's getting to be a vending machine. You put a nickel in and you get a reward. It doesn't lead people; it merely reflects their values." (This, it should be said, was spoken before the courageous act of unpopular and decisive leadership taken by the Roman Catholic archbishop in Louisiana who excommunicated three racists, including a political district leader, over their refusal to obey the prelate's school integration order. There is every indication that church leaders, by appealing to young people's courage rather than adapting themselves to their craving for comfort, could be a real rather than an illusory influence. The Reverend Dr. Martin Luther King has demonstrated this. And when Yale's chaplain, for example, joined the Freedom Riders in the South, he probably did more for organized religion than do all the arrangers of church socials combined.)

Without such toughness, the reaction is more apt to be like that of a Princeton student: "God, I think, must be a pretty nice guy." Since 84 per cent of today's teen-agers are church members and more than half attend church regularly, they could undoubtedly be influenced strongly by religious values. But if to the palship of parents and teachers, religion merely adds another "good guy," the effect is not likely to be crucial.

In their material goals, teen-agers appear to want pretty much what their parents want—only more and sooner. An alumnus of New York's City College, from which he graduated in the early forties, expressed shock after a recent return to a student function. He recalled the highly intellectual, intensely political attitude of students in his not-so-distant undergraduate years, as well as their cynical attitude toward material possessions and routine symbols of success and status. "Today, City College co-eds seem to talk only about that house in the suburbs—the kind of thing they used to ridicule the girls at expensive colleges for," he said.

The Gallup survey said that even if some of today's girls were romantic about sex, almost all of them were down-to-earth, specific and conventional about their dream houses. The little white home with the picket fence has been replaced by a $60,000 suburban ranch or Colonial house like the ones in the backgrounds of the automobile or soft-drink advertisements. A typical reply: "I would like an eight-room, two-story Colonial home: living room, dining room, kitchen, den and bath downstairs; master bedroom, guest room, two other bedrooms and bath upstairs. I would like the house to be white with a large front porch with four large white columns. I would like a drive that makes a semicircle and I would like to live in the country. I would like a typically Colonial living room with an enormous fireplace . . ."

Another girl describes an amazingly similar house, but with the added specifications of marble floors, a recreation room, crystal chandeliers and a swimming pool, "oval-shaped and not too large."

While the dream houses are specific, the younger generation's actual acquaintance with the economic facts of life appears sketchy. For, keeping in mind the specifications of real estate, it may come as something of a surprise to learn that the typical college boy expects to be earning about $12,000 at the age of forty; the male high school graduate, about $9,000 and the rest about $8,000. Yet the girls, despite their grandiose material dreams, actually expect their future husbands to earn about 20 per cent less than the boys themselves anticipate. The likelihood that such advertisement-inspired dreams, coupled with such appalling economic ignorance, will lead to disillusionment or marital disaster, or both, is uncomfortably great. At the very least, it supports the charge of the American Economics Association that entire generations of Americans have been permitted to grow up as economic illiterates. They are either entirely unaware of the laws and realities of economics because their schools fail to teach or require the subject, or they are taught by teachers who themselves have not had the benefit of actual instruction in economics. In the absence of knowledge, they become the innocent victims of economic seduction via advertisements and the never-never land of "Enjoy Now, Pay Later."

The confusion of values is further underlined by the results of a five-year study by two psychologists, Dr. Donald D. O'Dowd and Mr. David C. Beardslee. According to the testimony of 1,200 college students, the physician is the true hero of contemporary civilization in many teen-agers' eyes. Why? Not only because of the humane services he renders, but because he combines the twin ideals of high social status and high income. He is the only professional who can eat his cake and have it, too: perform valuable, respected service and still ride in a Cadillac. And yet, when modern teenagers find out that the attainment of this admirable status must be postponed for long years of arduous study, rough internship and low-paying residency, the attraction vanishes. The fact is that applications to medical schools have dropped to a dangerously low point in recent years. The sciences with quicker returns have crowded medicine out of glamour dreams.

The new interest in college admission and the competition for high test scores should not be mistaken for a great revival of respect for learning (although it is certainly an improvement over the earlier almost total contempt for scholarly achievement). A recent book called *The American College,* based on sociological research about undergraduate attitudes, charges that there has never been greater concern with getting into college, coupled with so little interest in actual learning. This may be excessively harsh, but there is enough evidence from other observers to prove the basic truth of the charge. James S. Coleman's study of adolescent culture indicates that schools in wealthy communities give little real status to academic achievement, despite high interest in college admission. The leading crowd of boys did not usually include top scholars, and the leading crowd of girls gave the academically distinguished members of their group almost equally little prominence.

It is interesting, too, that academic achievement through hard work rather than through the ease of natural brilliance tends to be scorned, even though similar success through extraordinary effort in athletics is held in high regard. In fact, the boy who overcomes natural handicaps to win a place on the team is likely to be a hero. The boy who tries as hard for intellectual distinction is a "grind." The student who gives up on his studies and turns instead to the cultivation of activities that make him "well-liked" is applauded; the classmate who fails to give his all in sports and "lets the school down" is the equivalent of the traitor.

When Father Theodore Hesburgh, the distinguished and scholarly president of the University of Notre Dame, tried to stress the importance of academic achievement and appeared, at least by implication, to give less priority to the football team, students picketed with a sign inscribed: "To Hell With Excellence." A similar sentiment appears to have been expressed by the girl who told the Gallup survey: "I don't want to be above normal. I want to be average. I have everything I want; I have security, clothes, love, a pet, a boy friend. I wanted a typewriter; I got a typewriter."

A boy said: "I don't want to be rich. I want just a little better than an average salary."

In a survey of sixteen-year-olds (by Havinghurst and Taba), a boy who hoped to be an engineer wrote: "I should like to be very healthy and have an electric tool shop in the basement as well as a boat in the river and short enough hours at work so I could use some of these privileges. Maybe I would be more satisfied if I owned a business of my own, small or large; it makes no difference."

According to the Gallup poll, almost 90 per cent of the youngsters are satisfied with their present lives—an interesting contrast with their protestations of feeling threatened by The Bomb and extinction whenever they get into trouble. One boy said: "I want something that's within my grasp, not something I can't reach."

It would be easy to blame the youngsters themselves, and this is generally what the older generation tries to do, thus evading its responsibilities. Those who are ready to take that easy escape from blame might listen to a young boy in Seattle: "Our parents led a tougher life. They fought a Depression and a war. And they've protected us. They've made sure that we have more than they had. We're pampered."

An Eastern college girl added: "Of course, we're soft. We got too much too soon."

A high-school student in California: "Goals? We've got no goals. Our parents have achieved them all for us."

Goals and values are tricky and evasive things to assess. When Coleman asked parents what they most wanted their children to achieve in school, he was told that having them become brilliant students headed the list. But, these same parents complained, this was not what the youngsters wanted. They, so the parental estimate went, would rather be athletic stars and cheerleaders. The rub is that when these same parents' children were asked the same question, they replied that they knew their parents would be happier to have daughters who were cheerleaders rather than science assistants and sons who made the basketball teams. Who is fooling whom? Or themselves? At least one point is clearly in the youngsters' favor: when it comes to admission to the "prestige" colleges, parents' pressure is more unreasonable than teen-agers' estimate of their own abilities. Similarly, it is the parents and teachers who generally complain about excessive academic pressures on the youngsters. In fact, a *Scholastic Magazine* survey showed that 72 per cent of the teen-agers queried said they would welcome a raising of academic standards in their schools. Only 22 per cent said they would resent this. Another survey indicated that 70 per cent of the youngsters wanted to see more stress placed on science; 66 per cent on mathematics; 65 per cent on foreign languages, and 56 per cent on English.

A fair conclusion is that youth, when talking in generalities, would like to be comfortable and without too much pressure of work; but when the discussion becomes more specific, young people are beginning to rebel against the low standards permitted by too many of their elders.

Perhaps he is not typical, but the Ivy League student who complained about a lack of challenge is finding more company among college undergraduates who are ready for more challenging work than they can find. At any rate, he reported: "I can honestly say that during my last three years at Princeton I have spent two fifths of my time on campus, two fifths away having a wonderful time, and the last fifth traveling back and forth. I have made trips annually to Florida or the Caribbean, and have had only one dateless weekend in three years. Yet with all this gallivanting about, I have managed to keep my academic grades well above average."

A boy in the Gallup poll said: "You know you'll get through high school—even if you never study. All you have to do is wait long enough. How can it have value?"

A girl, who might be quoted to parents and educators concerned about excessive academic pressure, said: "How many hours a year do we spend at pep rallies? Why don't we have learning rallies?"

The temptation is to talk about goals and attitudes in a vacuum. Few of those who complain that youth lacks direction and purpose question whether the absence of a basic foundation in solid knowledge may not be their most serious obstacle. Teachers and students are often so busy fulfilling requirements that they overlook the meaning and purpose of study. The key question for students is: "What are we responsible for?" And the question implies merely: "What is required of us to pass the tests to get into college to be assured of a good job?"

Ignorance of basic economics has already been pointed out. Ignorance of history is the inevitable road to ignorance about real and comparative values of civilization. In the Gallup survey, high school students stressed that they did not understand either the Soviet Union or the United States. A sixteen-year-old girl said: "I don't know enough about Communism to talk about it. Everybody says it's bad, but we're never told what it is. I think the people who want us to be better teen-agers should tell us what Communism is."

She gets support from a prominent adult authority. The Reverend William Coffin, Chaplain at Yale University, who was an Operation-Crossroads leader in Guinea, said: "We are reaping now what we sowed. We were afraid to study Marxism, or we dismissed it as a last-resort kind of thing. We never assessed its compelling emotional power." He charges that many American youths feel themselves incapable of debating Communism on foreign soil where some of the people have already begun to fall under its spell, in the absence of eloquent American spokesmen.

Communism is not the only area of ignorance. One survey found that about half of the college students in the United States still believe in primitive old wives' tales, such as the curing effects of whiskey or the influence of music on an unborn child. Surveys of high school students' ideas on health and hygiene find much of their "knowledge" to be based on television advertising claims—and just about as irrelevant to reality.

A study of American teen-agers by Remmers and Radler showed that despite the generally compulsory teaching of American history, a degree of either ignorance or indifference exists that can hardly be considered anything less than frightening. Forty-one per cent, for example, disagreed with the principles of a free press. A *Scholastic Magazine* survey about leisure-time reading found that none of the youngsters questioned could remember the author of *Tale of Two Cities*. About 90 per cent had forgotten the authors of *Gone With the Wind* and *Of Human Bondage*.

It is difficult, if not impossible, in a world of shoddy adult values and easy security for all but a small minority, to expect the majority of teen-agers to set high and exacting goals for themselves. It would be sheer hypocrisy to pretend that our daily pattern of life maps out a set of clear priorities for young people. In a welter of public (rather than personal) relations and symbols of status (rather than achievement) it is understandable that the primary goal is often pushed aside by trivialities.

Let the following therefore stand, not as a typical example but as the real-life parody of the danger. It is the story of a college student who decided to elope with his true love, after an Ivy League vacation in Florida. "With our last hundred dollars I went to buy our plane tickets back to Baltimore," he writes. "I noticed that for the same price we could go to Mexico City. We discussed the choice in a cocktail lounge but decided against it because we were both ill due to the seafood we had eaten the night before." Indigestion—the plague of affluence—put an end to dreams of glorious independence.

14 *Conclusions*

Adults of every era, from time immemorial, have been complaining about youth. As the years pass, the misdemeanors of the young appear more offensive. If the preceding chapters are interpreted as representing exasperation with today's adolescents, then they have been misread. The fault is not with youth; the errors are those of adult society. Teenagers behave exactly in the way they have been brought up to behave; they evolve the attitudes that are implicitly or explicitly expected; they aspire to goals and ideals which their elders inspire, or fail to inspire. Intrinsically, they are neither better nor worse than earlier generations. But both for their own good and that of society, now and in the future, they must be judged by their actions rather than by their potential.

There must be no misunderstanding about the examples of extreme behavior or aimlessness cited earlier in an effort to document a pattern. The reply will be made that many teen-agers are wonderful youngsters who honor and respect their parents, who would sooner die than steal cars or even drive them carelessly, who are more virtuous and more abstemious than their elders.

All this is true. But the pressures on the "good teen-agers" merely hasten the trends we have described and make it more difficult for thoughtful youngsters to resist both the pressures and their exploitation. No useful purpose is served either by complaining that young people "these days" are going to the dogs or, following the other extreme, of ignoring the facts and hoping for the best. Those communities which have, in the interest of good "public relations," ignored the handwriting on the wall, have merely invited trouble, including an increasing harvest of unmarried pregnancies. Those who complain that newspapers merely "play up" the scandals and unfavorable news overlook the fact that the presentation of good news does not prevent bad news from happening.

The easiest and most deceptive patent-medicine "solution" is to quote the ancient philosophers to prove that there is nothing new under the sun—so why worry. Among the favorite quotations is this one from Socrates: "Our youth now loves luxury. They have bad manners, contempt for authority, disrespect for their elders. Children nowadays are tyrants." The flaw in this reasoning is the conclusion that, since all these problems faced the Greeks so long ago, they cannot be serious today. It would be more to the point to ask: What happened to Greece? Or to Rome? Or to any civilization once it substituted self-indulgence for self-discipline?

In many ways, the temptation to meet problems with "inaction through understanding" is even greater today. Everybody is an amateur psychiatrist. So many people have analyzed the reasons for the problems of contemporary society that comprehension has replaced correction. This is reflected with tragi-comic regularity in the defense offered by juvenile delinquents: they have learned to play back to their elders all the Freudian reasons in all the social-work jargon to explain why they are in trouble through no fault of their own.

More often than not, they are right in their self-diagnosis. But diagnosis alone is useless—worse than useless if it is the key only to a fatalistic excuse that nothing can be done about it. In the worst cases, it adds self-pity, truculence, hostility toward society and a kind of smug enjoyment of heading for trouble on a course irrevocably fixed by somebody else. But if it is fixed on a collision course, the "somebody else" can do no more than pick up the pieces.

Many well-meaning observers in saying quite accurately that society is at fault are led to the conclusion that the only answer therefore is in a total reform of society. There can be no question that society could stand reforms and that some specific ones can be achieved even in the relatively short run. The worst excesses of commercial exploitation of teen-agers, and particularly the beaming of television advertising at infants, could be corrected by law, without any resort to censorship. The use and abuse of cars could be controlled. But these are relatively minor aspects of the problems.

To advocate grandiose reform plans of society as the basic steps in coping with the problems of adolescent society is to succumb to the pious parlor game played by after-dinner speakers and campaigning politicians: to map out grandiloquent goals which nobody opposes—or takes seriously.

The real problems of today's teen-agers can and must be tackled on more practical and less flamboyant levels of action. Society does not renew or reform itself by total, sweeping magic. Reformers, to accomplish anything, need the patience to take small steps toward limited improvement. They must know that while it is impossible to move mountains, much can be gained from the laborious digging of irrigation ditches. Instead of saying therefore that teen-age mores cannot be changed until society can be reformed, it is more realistic to begin the reshaping of society with youth. If in the process young people are inevitably confronted with shabby sights of adult mores, their elders can admit that what they see is wrong, but that this is no reason not to make a new start.

The editor of a high school newspaper recently offered a concise lesson. He said that when he was "very young," he was taught to think and believe everything about American life and history was perfect and flawless. A few years later, he went on, he did some reading on his own and concluded that everything he had been told had been lies and deception. His rebellion over such hypocritical betrayal led him to despise everybody. But finally, he said, he learned to discover more of the truth: there is much that is good and admirable along with a good deal that is shabby and distasteful in the American story (as there is in the story of mankind). He considered this quite acceptable. Far from shattering his faith, this discovery of perspective rebuilt his confidence and his sense of balance. He emerged neither starry-eyed nor disillusioned. But he wound up with a stinging message to his elders: Don't hide the truth, but teach it; don't substitute fairy tales for facts; don't confuse loyalty to ideals with blindness to faults.

The same lesson applies to the setting of standards. The present trend is one of trying to establish all-inclusive "codes," agree on them in community-wide forums and expect young people to conform to them. This may be a pleasant exercise and will make some well-intentioned people go home with a sense of accomplishment. But in most instances it just won't work. It won't work because it is organized and based on the false premise of togetherness in social reform. A popular magazine even tried to offer a "summer code" for sub-teen girls: "Get up for breakfast at 9:00, make own bed. One (1) dinner guest a week. Keep screen doors shut. Only two (2) lunch guests a week. Lunch at 12:30, dinner at 6:30. Only one overnight guest every two weeks. Keep room neat. Bathe every day. Set the table. . . . Feed the parakeet."

Society is not a resort hotel, and even resort hotels are rarely reformed by the innkeeper's code.

First to go should be the idea that everything must be "fun," with fun interpreted as the effortless accomplishment of something pleasant. The "fun ethic" itself is a barefaced fraud, and the fact that it has been sold to adults as well as teen-agers only makes it worse. In reality, of course, the reverse is usually the truth: most pleasant things must be accomplished by varying amounts of effort which can be exciting, stimulating or, at times, downright difficult and troublesome.

Entire industries and much of our public relations are based on the fraudulent notion that important goals can be achieved without effort. Real fun is a by-product, not an end in itself. There is no such thing as quick and easy learning. Every new theory of education is sold down the river by the fun fraud—the sugar-coated pill to easy mastery. Teaching machines and review books promise acceptance by "the college of your choice" and supermarkets sell teaching aids guaranteed to lead to scholastic success, through a series of fun-exercises.

A report in the *Saturday Evening Post,* entitled "How to Have Fun in the Hospital," tells how teen-agers in a special teen-age wing at Emmanuel Hospital in Portland, Oregon, are offered "unlimited snacks, jam sessions and wheel-chair drag races." Making a medical virtue of certain fun aspects of teen-age culture, the hospital permits—read: encourages—patients to "eat hot dogs and hamburgers day after day for lunch and supper."

There are strong indications that adolescents want to be treated as though they intended to grow up rather than as if the world owed them a permanent and separate adolescent isolation ward. Schools, hospitals, churches and, yes, the home, can (without being forbidding and unpleasant) maintain adult regulations, and still be considered friendly. Teenagers want to be treated with understanding, but they do not want all adults to be their pals. They need, and often want, mature strength to turn to. Too often they learn to their disappointment that the man they seek tries desperately to be "one of the boys" and so is of no help to them. An old-fashioned father said to us: "My son has lots of pals his own age, but he only has one father."

In a recent television interview, a group of high school drop-outs agreed that their most serious complaint about teachers was their soft desire to be liked. They said what they were looking for were teachers who had the courage to be hard and fair at the same time.

The mistake adults—parents and teachers—make is to take the wrong things seriously about young people. The old-fashioned "sophomore slump" in college, frequently caused by a combination of too much social activity (often encouraged by the freshman "view book" about college life) and too little self-discipline, has been analyzed into all kinds of serious problems. Thus, difficulties which could be solved with a little straightforward, friendly advice are labeled as an "identity crisis." The result is that youngsters expect to have problems and wait for somebody else to lead them into the promised land.

Henri Peyre writes in *Daedalus:* "Every adolescent has been treated as a network of problems and his neuroses or his whims have been surrounded with awe. The teacher of teen-agers enters the classroom as he would a psychiatric hospital; the parents, fearful of asserting their own influence on these youngsters in their critical state of metamorphosis, secretly trying to make themselves alike to their progeny, whose complexity and scorn for the elders baffle them, wring their hands in despair and pray that the adolescent may 'go steady' and thus find stability with a friend of the opposite sex, since he fails to discover it in the home. . . . Through treating every child and every teen-ager as a potentially unbalanced person, through evincing a ridiculous, punctilious respect for every manifestation of his personality and every mumbling of his self-expression (before there is much to be expressed), through our fear of stifling a potential Mozart or a Rimbaud in our schoolboys, we have failed to assist the child to develop into a man, to strive to become a leader."

We ask young people too often what they think we should do about them. By telling them that this is the "democratic" way, we not only make them believe it is wrong for adults to impose standards and set some rules and limitations, but we deprive them of meaningful guidance. Most adults appear torn between fear of the adolescents' awakening concern with sex and the desire to see them mated as early as possible. In the interest of scientific child-rearing, parents "enlighten" youngsters, long before they are interested, about the "natural functions" of sex—and then are surprised to find adolescents, without intellectual and emotional maturity, treating sex as just that—a routine function, like eating and exercise. American education, says Dr. Edward D. Eddy, Jr., President of Chatham College and one of the foremost students of youth's attitudes, has "fallen for the American desire to maintain youth in a state of perpetual puerility."

"In a misguided notion of what high school students want, the college describes in glowing terms the social life, athletics, and extra-curricular activities which await the eager freshman—and hints broadly that those women's colleges aren't too far away either," Dr. Eddy says.

Here, then, are some strong indications where reforms might start. If it is true, as Dr. Eddy continues, that "the American high school is now offering—in all its gory messiness—what used to be encountered in collegiate living," then the educational institutions must make the unpopular start. The stress on football or basketball, the marching bands, the drinking parties, the steady dating and queens of the balls, once part of the college culture, are now established in many high schools and are rapidly filtering down to the junior high schools.

This can be dealt with. There is no need to wait for society at large to mend its ways. A recent news photo showed a high school "belle" in a posh suburban Connecticut community attired in abbreviated chorus girl costume, ready to dance for the local Fathers' Club in a school-sponsored evening's entertainment. Youngsters at this age have enough inevitable concern about their sexual maturing without trying to imitate professional adult exhibitionism. Educators complain, and with reason, about the constant impact of sex-in-advertising, sex-in-magazines, sex-in-films; for the moment, there is little they can do about this; but the "If you can't lick them, join them" attitude makes no sense at all.

Schools can make a healthy start in reversing the abuses of public relations and advertising. Instead of bemoaning those abuses, it should be the teachers' task to educate youngsters to the point where sham and false glitter will influence them much less. We assume that education can and must teach adolescents how to distinguish harmful political and economic philosophies from those which benefit mankind. How much easier it should be to teach these same youngsters to laugh at the patent medicine advertisments which fly in the face of every simple fact of science and biology. A good basic course on human biology could be taught by simply showing the "errors" in those body diagrams which have six-way pills dissolve in the bloodstream. A lesson in both logic and ethics could be based on unspecified "comparisons" that detergent X washes clothes "20 per cent whiter." A study of relativity and probabilities could be written around the scare messages about the number of Americans who are said to fall victim every hour to this, that or the other threat. It might even be feasible to teach good taste in music by dissecting the lack of talent out of which press-agentry builds teen-age idols.

The possibilities are endless. All of them, however, require courage. To fly in the face of popular conventions, especially if they are firmly anchored in vested economic interests, is not without hazards. But those who are unwilling to swim against a current they know to be running in the wrong direction forfeit the right to complain about the destination of the other swimmers.

Some of the in-school reforms are even more basic. Year after year, news reports charge that there is much cheating in the schools. Educators generally reply that while the stories are probably exaggerated, academic cheating has always been a fact. This, too, is true. The question is whether fraud becomes more acceptable by being ancient. *Time* magazine told of a physician, Dr. Bryan Newsom, aged sixty-five, who since his college days has made a moderately profitable hobby of the ghostwriting of high school commencement speeches—both for student valedictorians and principals. The practice—or rather the demand for it—is unpleasant enough. But the shocking aspect of the story is that, according to *Time,* "most of his orders are signed by school principals, and more than half the checks he receives are drawn on school funds."

The to-be-anticipated excuse (which makes this a valid example) will be that ghosted speeches have long been part of American mores. But there is an answer to this apology: the technical speech writer who combines the information of many governmental and industrial departments is probably the only legitimate form of the ghost, a version of the researcher. Even if the don't-do-it-yourself way of public utterance has become widespread, there is no reason for the schools to perpetuate and sanction the practice. There is a considerable difference between the performance of a campaigning politician, who must confront a dozen or more audiences a day, and the valedictorian (or even the principal), who presumably is being asked to present, from the depth of his own convictions, a message of personal meaning and sentiment. If he has nothing to say, he should remain silent; if he is unable to say what he wants to say, then his rise to top standing in his class (or his profession) has been a fraud; if he lacks the time, he has shown that he is incapable of managing his affairs. On either count, he should be considered disqualified. Any camouflage of his lack of qualification merely sanctions the evils the schools ought to reform.

This applies in equal measure to the excesses so regularly linked with college athletics. Many of the best schools and colleges are guilty. Most of them tend to shift the blame to "society," or more specifically to the tyranny of the alumni and potential donors. None of these excuses are acceptable. If education has a task of leadership and reform, the place to begin is at home, not in the self-righteous convention speeches and scholarly journals. The simple fact is that college football can be, and often is, as crassly commercial as the Madison Avenue approach to salesmanship that is so regularly attacked from the Ivory Tower.

Reforms require the courage to make unpopular decisions and uphold them. While this is not easy, there have been examples to prove that it is not impossible. In 1961, a faculty committee of Ohio State University demonstrated that it can be done—even against overwhelming opposition. It did so by voting against participation by the university's football team in the Rose Bowl contest.

An understanding of the courage involved in that decision

requires knowledge of the background of the institution as one of the outstanding football schools, not only within the Big Ten but in the nation. The total "take" of a Rose Bowl game can come close to a million dollars (although only a small fraction of this goes to the institutions involved). Yet against these facts and against violent reaction by students, alumni, townspeople and the football-obsessed local press, the faculty stood firm. The issue was whether the teachers responsible for the academic standing of the university could control its destiny and determine its purposes. They took their stand against what they considered the commercialism of an exhibition game and all the non-academic frenzy that surrounds it.

If the schools have a responsibility to start the reforms without waiting for society, parents must be expected to show the same strength and independence. The coward's way is to let adolescent society be run by public-opinion poll and the slogan, "But, Mom, everybody does it."

"This is the plea of the seventh-grader who wants to wear lipstick, and her teen-age brother who wants to borrow the family car," writes *New York Times* reporter Martin Tolchin. "It is the protest of the fourteen-year-old who is not allowed week-night dates, and of the sixteen-year-old who must be home before midnight."

What should parents do? Some may look at the Yonkers, New York, survey of high school juniors and seniors, which showed that the majority (58 per cent) drank alcoholic beverages and (64 per cent) drove the family car, and still say that unless their children are permitted to do what the majority is doing, they will be unpopular and frustrated. Reporter Tolchin, investigating the effect of the Yonkers survey, points out that some parents are doing exactly that. The mother of a teen-age girl, after hearing that most of her daughter's friends go to parties after evening church meetings at other youngsters' homes and stay out until two or three o'clock in the morning, said: "If my daughter had to be home early, she wouldn't be part of the group. If you're really going to be part of the group of kids, you have to be part of what they're doing."

By much the same reasoning, Coleman points out, the new girl in school "feels a need for a cashmere sweater, not merely to keep up with the others, but to establish her position." Parents then feel that partly to assure their daughter's status, partly to maintain the proper position in the competitive community for themselves, they must comply.

There is no point in either complaining that this is expensive and undesirable or in waiting for "society" to change its ways. Changes can only be made by individual families. Even the currently popular community meetings to agree on such matters as curfew, attire, parties, etc. are at best an illusion and, at worst, the road to another set of group standards. They are an illusion because the meetings are usually attended largely by those who want a change and ignored by those who most urgently need to change their ways. Even more important is the fact that merely adopting a different kind of jointly-arrived-at group compromise is not the same as coming to grips with the basic issue.

That issue is whether individual familes can regain the independence needed to raise young people, not for a mythical, uniform way of life but for the realities of personal (and far from uniform) lives to be led at different levels of interests and affluence. Short of the English school uniform (which may be more democratic, in the final analysis, than the suburban competition for uniform dress-symbols of affluence), no agreements on attire, for instance, will accomplish any real reform.

The only thing that can save parents from the strait jacket of living up to the Joneses is their own strength of character in raising their children with an understanding of differences in wealth. A parent must teach a child and later an adolescent that there is no shame in not being able to afford that cashmere sweater. How early in children's lives the damage is now being done and how far down the ladder the reform must therefore be set in motion was demonstrated by sixth-grade teacher Sophie Jaffe's report to the American Federation of Teachers.

"Children must learn as children that one cannot have everything one wants; that money and material abundance are not the acme of American democracy," she said. "Children today have television sets in their bedrooms, carry portable transistor radios to school and at home have only to make their desires known to have them satisfied," she added. "On school field trips they brag about the money they spend."

In addition to having the courage to set their own standards without submitting blindly to herd pressures, parents as well as schools must be brave enough to establish rules and set limits for their own children, without waiting for society or even the community to reach an agreement. If they do so, they may learn to their surprise that adolescents really want such limitations and a clear understanding of how far they can go. Since teen-agers are uncertain about their actions and their maturity, they will, if left without regulations, keep probing and, in the absence of brakes, run into trouble. They will follow the group. The adolescent question to mother, "Don't you trust me?" asked with the proper dash of teen-age drama and hurt, needs often to be answered: "I trust you on your own, but not when you think you must be part of the crowd." A properly chaperoned teen-age party, for example, is not an insult to young people any more than the presence of law-enforcement officers in even the most orderly community.

At a teen-age convention of the Wayne County Camp Association, the youngsters agreed that "teen-agers are punished by being pampered," and that they are "led to become accustomed to too much to soon." In an essay contest sponsored by the Attorney General of New York State, 64 per cent of more than ten thousand students in public, private and parochial high schools said that the automobile, television, "social obligations and parental pampering" have made them academically and physically soft.

Fortunately there are growing indications that intelligent teen-agers are ready for a rebellion against the tinsel of *nouveau riche* affluence. Martin Tolchin reported in the *New York Times* that two teen-age "companies" are preparing to set up off-Broadway theaters with original productions protesting the pap that is being dished out to youngsters commercially. In planning shows for children, one of the young producers said: "We don't think it would be so terrible if they went out with a few more ideas than they had when they entered, and a larger vocabulary."

What kind of ideas? Well, for one thing there is to be a revue in which three flannel-suited witches would chant:

> "Thrice the Univac hath spoke:
> Sell your goods to younger folk;
> Thrice its tubes and tapes did purr:
> Make each kid a customer;

Thrice its twanging clocks have struck:
Bobby-socks have got the buck."

This may well be a hint of a dissatisfaction with the status quo that could be nurtured into constructive insurrection.

Dr. Charles Frankel of Columbia University said at the 1962 Conference of the Child Study Association that the lack of clear off-limits rules has deprived youth of an important privilege—to rebel. "It is hard to rebel if everybody understands you so well," he said. "Children like their parents, but they worry if Dad never gets mad. There should be a clear limit or frontier where children end and parents begin."

It will take both schools and parents to reverse the long-standing trend of permissiveness as a doctrine, proclaimed in a misguided notion of democracy. "I know quite a few parents who are nothing short of authoritarian in their application of permissiveness," says Dr. Frankel. And Professor Robert Ulich of Harvard University adds an appeal to parents and teachers to understand that the difficult business of growing up demands "not only freedom from false security, but also respect for rightful authority."

And it is equally important that parents once again permit their children to act like children. The pressure on youngsters to grow up socially is nothing short of obscene. Attempts to reverse the trend cannot be left to society" as a unit. For one thing, the present unnatural hothouse growth is too profitable for too many commercial interests. It is up to parents to call a halt and up to the schools to lead the way.

Instead of feeling guilty about interfering with precocious maturity, parents should take the advice of such respected experts as Dr. Benjamin Spock, who said in a *Ladies' Home Journal* article: "Some children who aren't ready at all are forcing themselves to compete for partners and to play the roles of people in love." It is time for sensible parents to take a strong stand against mothers who try match-making for their elementary school girls, just as it is time to discourage misguided parents from thinking about admission to a prestige college the moment they send their children to be "tested" for selective admission to nursery school.

A sensible mother, Mrs. Cleo McNelly in Cleveland, says, in discussing her twelve-year-old daughter: "We owe it to our children to be unpopular with them sometimes. They have a right on occasion to think we are heels. When pressure is on them to join their group in something they know they shouldn't do, they should be able to say, 'I'd be glad to go along, but my parents are heels. They won't let me.' "

But more is needed than parental and educational courage in defining sensible rules and acceptable behavior. Teen-agers need two growing-up aids, and need them badly: the first is a sense of purpose which permits them entry into the maturity of being needed and taken seriously, not according to bust size but measured by standards of mind and training; the second is an awareness of fine adult "examples" whom they can imitate.

It is hard for teen-agers to feel a sense of personal influence in the world today. Joan Wallach, a student at Brandeis University, writes in a letter to the *New York Times Magazine:* "Students have no commitment to political parties because the parties themselves remain uncommitted in politics. But when both political parties are willing to compromise the very principles students seek, they cannot but be disillusioned and cynical about the efficacy of working through these parties."

This is neither an atypical nor an unreasonable complaint. Under the shadow of the Big Bomb, Big Labor, Big Government and Big Industry—not to mention the even Bigger Government of the Communist world—students and teen-agers in general would be unrealistic indeed if they did not sense how little influence their efforts will wield, if they expected total, general reforms and victories.

This is exactly why such pinpointed movements as the Peace Corps, Operation-Crossroads Africa, the anti-discrimination lunch counter sit-ins, the Freedom Rides and the nuclear test-ban demonstrations have caught on so rapidly.

Reports from college campuses across the country by *New York Times* reporter Nan Robertson gave powerful evidence that youth, given a sense of purpose and mission, can rise above the tawdry climate of commercialism and expediency. When fourteen students from Grinnell College in Iowa, an institution without any fighting traditions, held a three-day "peace fast" in front of the White House, a hundred others joined the hunger demonstration on campus and almost half of all students attended a chapel meeting to honor the Washington contingent. Within a startlingly short time, the trip by the little group of activists inspired students from Iowa, Minnesota, and as far away as New England to go to the capital.

"We were building up to explode out of the private world of college," said Larry Smucker of Bluffton, Ohio. "We wanted to assert our feelings and our intellectual arguments in a more public way."

Another student added: "It was a symbolic act, not a stunt. We knew that we could do it, but that it would be uncomfortable."

Readiness to "explode out of" the private world of youth —even at the risk of discomfort—is a good start toward maturity.

It seems paradoxical that the extreme right-wing movement has captured the imagination of at least a minority of student activists. But there are good reasons. Liberalism in both major parties is cautious, tame and respectable. Left-wing extremism could, in view of Soviet aims, power and performance, attract only the perversely immature. The only outrageous and iconoclastic rebellion left for young "revolutionaries" is that of the ultra-conservative. Since most of today's youth has only the sketchiest idea of the Great Depression and the role of the conservative laissez-faire doctrine in bringing it about, the bravado of right-wing youngsters is not inhibited by rational consideration of the consequences.

To find new heroic examples for young people today, we must first get over a misguided pseudo liberal attitude that spread in the twenties and thirties. Hero worship, particularly in history and literature in and out of school, was considered a mark of reaction. Young people were encouraged to debunk their heroes; the personal approach to history was played down, if not virtually omitted, in favor of a study of social currents.

But adolescents need heroes. If heroes are not offered to them, they will create their own, as they have managed to do with such dismal results as the teen-age idols of Rock 'n' Roll.

Those who say that reform can only come by way of example are, of course, right. But if they add that, with society corrupt and lacking in personal greatness among its leaders, there can be no reform until all of society—the local politicians, the parents, the teachers, everybody—

provides examples, then they hold out nothing but defeatism and despair. Examples must be offered, not by a miraculously purified society but by men worthy of admiration and respect.

This is not a plea for a return to the unquestioning, chauvinistic worship of national heroes. Quite probably, the swing of the pendulum from the extreme of jingoistic hero worship to the smashing of all images of greatness was the result of a lack in critical intelligence among the extremists of both sides. Young people are strong enough to accept their heroes as human beings, with flaws and shortcomings. This is part of an understanding of humanity and of history, and to camouflage it with fairy-tale perfection is self-defeating.

James Reston wrote in the *New York Times:* "The examples placed before a nation are vital. What we constantly observe, we tend to copy. What we admire and reward, we perpetuate. This is why John Glenn himself is almost as important as his flight into outer space, for he dramatized before the eyes of the whole nation the noblest qualities of the human spirit."

And if such examples are vital to the nation, they are doubly important to teen-agers.

Mr. Reston observed Colonel Glenn returning from his historic voyage and "when he came back and saw his lovely wife, Annie, he put his head on her shoulder and cried. Thereafter nothing ruffled him, not the President, or the clamorous press, or the whirring of cameras, or the eager, shouting crowds."

New models and styles are set daily by television, Mr. Reston says, but most of them are models of cars and styles of dresses and hairdos. The youth of a nation needs something more heroic as a model—a Gettysburg Address, or a Churchillian oration, or the daring flight of a Lindbergh, or the quiet courage of a Pasternak.

The memorable performance of Colonel Glenn "may not stamp out juvenile delinquency overnight, but the models of the nation—not the uncovered cover girls of today but the larger models of human character—are probably more important than this age believes."

Not all the models can or must be national in scope. Good teachers and strong parents can provide an image that makes the phony mass culture of the vulgar and untalented teen-age idols fade. Adolescents are not insensitive, provided they are given a sense of values.

There is no mystery in the strong impact which science has made on young people. The sciences spell excitement, discovery, power of the mind. The laboratory is a proving ground for competence. The science teacher is not a pal but the key to knowledge and experimentation. He is respected, not for trying to buy popularity, but for his ability and experience. A good science teacher symbolizes everything adult society ought to mean to the adolescent. He has no need to bribe the young by stepping down to their level because it is clearly understood that he lives by what he knows and is inspired by his thirst for knowing more.

There will be outraged protests that this sets science apart and that it is a slur on the teachers of the humanities and the arts. Not at all. There is no reason why teachers in other fields cannot and should not be equally successful in capturing the imagination of youth. All they need is a similar sense of purpose and pride in the power of their own fields of study. A classicist can be as close to the teen-ager's search for purpose and identity as the nuclear physicist. But he must be as hard and serious about his effort—and as loath to try to defraud young people by offering them sugar-coated pabulum in order to prove that "learning can be fun." Those who try to "sell" religion or even religious philosophy by making God the benevolent patron of bingo games will only send young people in search of more powerful heroes. Dr. Eddy quotes students as saying: "We don't want a comfortable faith, bending to please our little likes or dislikes. We want rigidity, and we will respect the rigidity of others. . . . We do not want our religious faith nurtured by a saccharine diet of prune-whip tolerance."

Spiritually or academically, the reforms require a certain toughness of mind and standards. This should not be confused with the selfish toughness of the ultra-conservatives, who would turn the schools into limited trade schools for the many and into college-preparatory academies for a privileged few. Toughness of mind should lead to self-discipline rather than to a lack of compassion for others. Above all, it should put competence and effort on a pedestal.

Dr. Friedenberg concludes in *The Vanishing Adolescents:* "By helping the adolescent develop good, specific reasons for thinking well of himself, the school can contribute greatly to a stable identity. These reasons are competences, and adolescents with the help of good teachers can become very competent in mind, heart, and body. . . . School ought to be a place where you can not only learn to *be* a scholar, a fighter, a lover, a repairman, a writer, or a scientist, but learn that you are *good* at it, and in which your awareness and pride in being good at it becomes a part of your sense of being you."

Dr. Carl F. Hansen, Superintendent of Schools in the District of Columbia, who has initiated some tough-minded reforms in his school system, expresses the same thought slightly differently. "Too many students and too many adults have acquired a 'get-by' attitude toward their work as a result of school experiences," he said. "It is time to restore dependable craftsmanship to a place of respect . . . and the primary school is unquestionably one place to begin."

Perhaps commitment is the key word. The models and the heroes of young people must be committed so that they can inspire commitment. The Peace Corps or the fight for urban renewal or for civil rights require commitment. The wish to succeed at a job or a profession or a research project, even if it means postponing marriage and economic security, demands commitment, often sure to appear imprudent to the security-minded adults. The director of volunteers at Beverly Hospital in Beverly, Massachusetts, tells of the commitment of hundreds of teen-age volunteers who help with tough and important chores—an ironic contrast with the teen-age hospital wing where wheel-chair drag races are encouraged so that being a patient, too, will be "fun."

There are strong indications that the tightening of academic standards in the schools and the new competition for scholastic achievement is regarded by many teen-agers as liberation rather than pressure. The students who are, in increasing number, "rating" their teachers and appraising the requirements of their schools may not be the darlings of the faculties they criticize; but they are putting a premium on quality—the quality of their own education. There is poetic justice in this trend: students appear to be telling their elders to stop trying to be nice guys. Perhaps, if adults lack the courage, the most able teen-agers will insist that the line be drawn—between adolescents and real (not just chronological) adults.

These able, thoughtful youngsters may be a minority, but they deserve all the help they can be given. If teen-age culture needs to lean on models, the leadership of the best among the teen-agers can be an important influence. In the past, it has been left without much aid from the adult world, in part because mediocre adults (including parents and teachers) are afraid of able, demanding and independent adolescents.

But these are the teen-agers who can break the teen-age tyranny over American society. They can laugh, not only at the teen-age idols but at the permanently adolescent adults, their Twist parties and their prestige-hunting.

Today these "committed" teen-agers may still be the equivalent of a government-in-exile. What they need, however, is not just crumbs of "foreign aid" from the adult community. They must be made interns in the adult world, not just ambassadors from the Disneyland of "adolescent society."

This must mean, too, that the concept of "well-roundedness" in education, with its invitation to dabbling without probing, must give way to an encouragement of consuming interests and passions. Teen-age advice books, faced with young people's precociously but irrevocably aroused sexual restlessness, usually have nothing better to offer than a brisk workout in the gym or on the ball field. There is a more fundamental answer in some artificial respiration for the life of the mind and a workout for the intellect.

This does not mean that the emotions should be slighted. But young people awakened to the greatness of the mind and inspired by admirable models of humanity are less likely to be as obsessed with personal emotions and problems as are so many of their peers and their elders today.

The young man or woman who has learned to be passionate about vital issues and problems is far less likely to become the prisoner of his misunderstood personal drives and undisciplined appetites—even in a society that has succumbed to these selfish preoccupations.

For several decades now, the most insecure and most immature members of adult society have permitted, often in the name of self-expression and pseudo psychology, the most insecure and most immature adolescents to establish their own independent and sovereign culture: teen-age. The task now is to make it clearly understood that adolescence is a stage of human development, not an empire or even a colony. The mission of the adult world is to help teen-agers becomes adults by raising their standards and values to maturity rather than by lowering adulthood to their insecure immaturity. The task for the adult world is to make adolescence a step toward growing up, not a privilege to be exploited.

Bibliography

The Adolescent in Your Family. Children's Bureau Publication 347. Washington, D.C., United States Department of Health, Education and Welfare, 1955.

BACON, SELDON D. "What Should You Teach Your Child About Drinking?" *McCall's* October, 1961.

BARUCH, DOROTHY W. *How To Live With Your Teen-Ager.* New York, McGraw-Hill, 1953.

BETTELHEIM, BRUNO. "The Problem of Generations." *Daedalus,* Winter, 1962.

BLACK, HILLEL. *Buy Now, Pay Later.* New York, William Morrow, 1960.

BOONE, PAT. *'Twixt Twelve and Twenty.* New Jersey, Prentice-Hall, 1958.

BOROFF, DAVID. "Among the Fallen Idols, Virginity, Chastity and Repression." *Esquire,* July, 1961.

BRODERICK, CARLFRED B. "New Data on Dating." *The PTA Magazine,* December, 1961.

BRYANT, BERNICE. *Miss Behavior.* New York, Bobbs-Merrill, 1948.

BUTZ, OTTO (ed.). *The Unsilent Generation.* New York, Rinehart, 1958.

CHILD STUDY ASSOCIATION OF AMERICA. Report, 38th Annual Conference, March 12, 1962.

CHRISTENSEN, HAROLD T. "Adolescence: Mystery, Madness or Milestone?" *The PTA Magazine,* September, 1961.

COLEMAN, JAMES S. *The Adolescent Society.* Glencoe, Free Press, 1961.

COURSEN, HERBERT R., JR. "The Continuing Relevance of Good Teaching." *The Independent School Bulletin,* May, 1962.

DAVIDSON, BILL. "Bobby Darin and Paul Anka: Boy Wonders—But Why?" *McCall's,* October, 1961.

DENNEY, REUEL. "American Youth Today: A Bigger Cast, A Wider Screen." *Daedalus,* Winter, 1962.

———, RIESMAN, DAVID, and GLAZER, NATHAN. *The Lonely Crowd.* New York, Anchor, 1953.

DORESS, DR. IRVING. "The Problem of Early Marriage." *The Bulletin on Family Development,* Spring, 1961.

DUNSING, MARILYN. "Teen-Agers—The Ad Man's Target." *The PTA Magazine,* October, 1961.

DUVALL, EVELYN MILLS. *The Art of Dating.* New York, Permabooks, 1960.

———. *Facts of Life and Love For Teen-Agers.* New York, Association Press, 1956.

EDDY, DR. EDWARD D., JR. Address at Fifteenth Annual Meeting of the National Association of College and University Chaplains at Moravian College. Bethlehem, Pennsylvania, April 26, 1962.

EGAN, PAUL J., and STRANG, RUTH. "Teen-Age Readers." *The PTA Magazine,* June, 1961.

ERIKSON, ERIK H. "Youth: Fidelity and Diversity." *Daedalus,* Winter, 1962.

FEDDER, RUTH. *You, the Person You Want to Be.* New York, McGraw-Hill, 1957.

FLETCHER, HELEN JILL, and HARTOGS, DR. RENATUS. *How to Grow Up Successfully.* New York, Bobbs-Merrill, 1961.

FRIEDENBURG, EDGAR Z. *The Vanishing Adolescent.* Boston, Beacon Press, 1959.

FRIGGENS, PAUL. "Let's Stop These High School Graduation Nightmares!" *The PTA Magazine,* April, 1961.

GALLUP, DR. GEORGE, and HILL, EVAN. "Youth: The Cool Generation." *Saturday Evening Post,* December, 1961.

———. "Shapping the 60's . . . Foreshadowing the 70's." *Ladies' Home Journal,* January, 1962.

GILBERT, EUGENE. *Advertising and Marketing to Young People.* Pleasantville, Printers Ink Books, 1957.

———. "Why Today's Teen-Agers Seem So Different." *Harper's,* November, 1959.

GLAZER, NATHAN, DENNEY, REUEL, and RIESMAN, DAVID. *The Lonely Crowd.* New York, Anchor, 1953.

GOODMAN, PAUL. *Growing Up Absurd.* New York, Random House, 1960.

GRAFTON, SAMUEL. "When Youth Runs Wild." *McCall's,* April, 1962.

GUITAR, MARY ANNE. "The Cautious Crusaders." *Mademoiselle,* August, 1961.

HANSON, EARL H. "Teen-Age Marriages." *National Education Association Journal,* September, 1961.

HARTOGS, DR. RENATUS, and FLETCHER, HELEN JILL. *How to Grow Up Successfully.* New York, Bobbs-Merrill, 1961.

HAVINGHURST, R. J., and TABA, H. *Adolescent Character and Personality.* New York, John Wiley, 1949.

HAYDEN, THOMAS. "Who Are the Student Boat-Rockers?" *Mademoiselle,* August, 1961.

HILL, EVAN, and GALLUP, DR. GEORGE. "Youth: The Cool Generation." *Saturday Evening Post,* December, 1961.

———. "Shaping the 60's . . . Foreshadowing the 70's." *Ladies' Home Journal,* January, 1962.

HOLLINGSHEAD, A. B. *Elmtown's Youth.* New York, Science Editions, 1961.

INHELDER, BARBEL, and PIAGET, JEAN. *The Growth of Logical Thinking From Childhood to Adolescence.* Translated by ANNE PARSONS and STANLEY MILGRAM. New York, Basic Books, 1958.

INGE, WILLIAM. *Splendor in the Grass.* New York, Bantam Books, 1961.

JOHNSON, ERIC W. *How to Live Through Junior High School.* New York, J. B. Lippincott, 1959.

Juvenile Delinquency. U.S. Senate, Committee on the Judiciary Report. Washington, D.C., Government Printing Office, August 8, 1961.

KEATS, JOHN. "College Marriage." *Glamour,* August, 1961.

KEMENY, JOHN G. "Needed: Well-Rounded Colleges." *New York Times Magazine,* March 25, 1962.

KENISTON, KENNETH. "Social Change and Youth in America." *Daedalus,* Winter, 1962.

KOHNER, FREDERICK. *Gidget Goes Hawaiian.* New York, Bantam Books, 1961.

KOMAIKO, JEAN R. "The Plight of Pregnant Teen-Agers." *Parents' Magazine,* January, 1962.

LANDERS, ANN. *Since You Ask Me.* New Jersey, Prentice-Hall, 1961.

LEITCH, DAVID. "The Salinger Myth." *Mademoiselle,* August, 1961.

LITTLE, VIVIAN. "Adolescents Are Human Beings Too." *The Clearing House,* November, 1961.

MACDONALD, DWIGHT. "Profile of Eugene Gilbert." *New Yorker,* November 22 & 29, 1958.

MACE, DR. DAVID. "Let's Abolish Dating Under Fifteen." *McCall's,* August, 1961.

MCGOWAN, WILLIAM N. "What's Happening in California Secondary Schools?" *Journal of Secondary Education,* December, 1961.

MALLERY, DAVID. *High School Students Speak Out.* New York, Harper, 1962.

MEAD, MARGARET. *And Keep Your Powder Dry.* New York, William Morrow, 1942.

———. *Male and Female.* New York, William Morrow, 1949.

———. "Stolen: Childhood . . ." Associated Press, 1961.

———. "Undergraduate Marriage—Yes or No?" *Carnegie Alumnus,* November, 1960.

MENNINGER, WILLIAM C. *How to Be a Successful Teenager.* New York, Sterling, 1954.

MORGENSTERN, DR. JOHN J. "Teen-Age Dating Patterns." *Na-*

tional Education Association Journal, January, 1961.
New Trends in Youth Organizations: A Comparative Survey. UNESCO Report. Paris, UNESCO, 1960.
NOVAK, MICHAEL. "God in the Colleges." *Harper's,* October, 1961.
OPPENHEIM, GARRETT. "Teen-Age Drinking Can Spell Disaster." *Parents' Magazine,* October, 1961.
PARSONS, TALCOTT. "Youth in the Context of American Society." *Daedalus,* Winter, 1962.
PEYRE, HENRI. "Has Western Europe Any Lessons For Us?" *Daedalus,* Fall, 1961.
PIAGET, JEAN, and INHEILDER, BARBEL. *The Growth of Logical Thinking From Childhood to Adolescence.* Translated by ANNE PARSONS and STANLEY MILGRAM. New York, Basic Books, 1958.
PURTELL, THELMA C. *The Intelligent Parents' Guide to Teen-Agers.* New York, Paul S. Eriksson, 1961.
———. "Maybe an Allowance Isn't Such a Good Idea." *Today's Living,* November 26, 1961.
RABINOVITCH, DR. RALPH. "Psychology of Adolescence." *Pediatric Clinics of North America, Adolescence,* February, 1960.
RADLER, D. H., and REMMERS, H. H. *The American Teen-ager.* New York, Bobbs-Merrill, 1957.
RAFERTY, GERALD. "Mayonnaise Yet!" *Today's Living,* September 10, 1961.
RATTNER, JOAN. "U.S. Kids Make Fads the Fashion." *This Week,* July 23, 1961.
REMMERS, H. H., and RADLER, D. H. *The American Teen-ager.* New York, Bobbs-Merrill, 1957.
RIDER, A. HAGGARD. "Stop the World, I'm Getting Off." *Columbia Owl,* March 28, 1962.
RIEFF, PHILIP. "The Mirage of College Politics." *Harper's,* October, 1961.
RIESMAN, DAVID. "Where Is the College Generation Headed?" *Atlantic Monthly,* April, 1961.
———, DENNEY, REUEL, and GLAZER, NATHAN. *The Lonely Crowd.* New York, Anchor, 1953.
SALINGER, J. D. *Catcher in the Rye.* New York, New American Library, 1951.
SANFORD, NEVITT. *The American College.* New York, John Wiley, 1962.
SCANLON, JOHN. "The Scent of Roses." *Saturday Review,* April 21, 1962.
SCHLEMAN, HELEN B., and STRATTON, DOROTHY C. *Your Best Foot Forward.* New York, McGraw-Hill, 1955.
SHULMAN, MAX. *I Was a Teen-Age Dwarf.* New York, Bantam, 1960.
"Sight and Sound." McCall's, October, 1961.
SPOCK, DR. BENJAMIN. "Disturbing Influences in Adolescence." *Ladies' Home Journal,* February, 1962.

STRANG, RUTH, and EGAN, PAUL J. "Teen-Age Readers." *The PTA Magazine,* June, 1961.

STRATTON, DOROTHY C., and SCHLEMAN, HELEN B. *Your Best Foot Forward.* New York, McGraw-Hill, 1955.

TABA, H., and HAVINGHURST, R. J. *Adolescent Character and Personality.* New York, John Wiley, 1949.

TAYLOR, FRANK J. "How to Have Fun in the Hospital." *Saturday Evening Post,* October 28, 1961.

UNGER, ART (ed.). *Datebook's Complete Guide to Dating.* New Jersey, Prentice-Hall, 1960.

"*Vogue's* Eye View of the Twist Toward Jazzy Boites." *Vogue,* November 15, 1961.

WEINSTEIN, GEORGE. "Our Senseless High School Secret Societies." *Coronet,* October, 1961.

"The Wild Ones." *The Times* (London) *Educational Supplement,* August 5, 1960.

WYLIE, LAURENCE. "Youth in France and the United States." *Daedalus,* Winter, 1962.

"You Are the Teenage Consumer." *Teen Times,* November, 1961.

Index